Detail Study of Phrases, Clauses & Sentences, including Idioms & Phrasal Verbs

Classification of Phrases, Clauses & Sentences with Illustrations & Examples

Mr. Peter

Made with ❤ on the Notion Press Platform

www.notionpress.com

DEDICATION

Dedicated to all my beloved school children

Writer's Academic works:

1. Study of Nouns, Pronouns, Adjectives & Articles (detail study) ISBN: 979-842-211-856-4 / 979-888-704-109-4
2. All about Verbs (Forms, Functions, Conjugation, Tense, Voice Change, Forming Questions & Negation) ISBN: 979-840-441-149-2 / 979-888-704-411-8
3. Study of Adverbs, Prepositions, Conjunctions & Interjections ISBN: 979-840-785-010-6 / 979-888-704-532-0
4. Detail Study of Phrases, Clauses & Sentences, including Idioms & Phrasal Verbs ISBN: 979-840-881-405-3 / 979-888-704-582-5
5. Study of Subject-Verb Agreement, Narration Change, Use of Punctuation; including Analysis, Synthesis & Split-up (Study through charts, division, explanation and examples) ISBN: 979-880-723-013-3 / 979-888-704-674-7
6. **Peter's 'English Grammar, A Complete Version of English Grammar,** (detail study, explanation & examples) ISBN: 979-879-725-020-3 / 979-888-704-463-7
7. **Question Bank of English Grammar & Composition (Learn through Exercises)** ISBN: 979-883-531-890-2 / 979-888-733-132-4
8. **Rhetoric & Prosody** (A handbook of Figures of Speech, rhymes, feet of poetic lines for High School Students) ISBN: 979-840-526-645-9 / 979-888-684-952-3
9. Picture Composition: For Primary Level, Std-I to V (Development of Writing Skill from Single Sentence Formation to Paragraph Writing, incl. question patterns and answer guide) ISBN: 979-888-805-249-5 (B&W) / 979-888-783-066-7 (color print)
10. Steps to Composition (Development of Writing Skill, Part-1), includes Picture Composition, Essay & Story Writing ISBN: 979-884-408-069-2 / 979-888-805-001-9
11. Development of Writing Skill, Part-2 (includes Letter Writing- Business Letters, Application for Jobs, Letters to Editor, bank authorities, Institutional Heads & others) ISBN: 979-835-689-886-0 / 979-888-833-455-3
12. Development of Writing Skill, Part-3 (includes- E-mails, Poster Making, Notices, Processing, Dialogue, Article, Speech & Debate Writing as well as Diary entry, Summary and Reporting) ISBN: 979-836-392-249-7 / 979-888-869-544-9
13. **A Book of Advanced Writing Skill, the Complete Version** (incl Part-1, 2 & 3) ISBN: 979-836-472-826-5 / 979-888-869-835-8

Author page URL's:

https://www.amazon.com/author/mr.peter

https://www.amazon.in/~/e/B09QW2P4TY *(For Indians, this and next)*

https://notionpress.com/store/s?NP_Books%5Bquery%5D=Mr.+Peter

https://www.amazon.co.uk/~/e/B09QW2P4TY

https://www.amazon.de/~/e/B09QW2P4TY

https://www.amazon.fr/~/e/B09QW2P4TY

https://www.amazon.co.jp/~/e/B09QW2P4TY

https://www.amazon.es/~/e/B09QW2P4TY

https://www.amazon.it/~/e/B09QW2P4TY

https://www.amazon.com.br/kindle-dbs/entity/author?asin=B09QW2P4TY

For Readers from India and nearby, you may place order with notionpress.com
Visit notionpress.com and type 'Mr. Peter' in the search box; give order of books to **avail elegant discounts** *using the following* **Coupon Codes;** as, unique00, bulk00, Deal1 and so on against the books: (if not work, contact to https://www.facebook.com/profile.php?id=100081822070172 or (5) Books Campaigns, Free Coupons, Learning English Grammar & Composition | Facebook

Coupon Codes	Book Name	Buy for	Discount %	Rebate Prices
unique00	**Advanced Writing Skill, the Complete Version** (incl. Part-1, 2 & 3)	1 copy	15	~~780~~ 663
PujaDeal10	Development of Writing Skill, Part-3	1 copy	18	~~365~~ 300
PujaDeal9	Development of Writing Skill, Part-2	1 copy	18	~~365~~ 300
PujaDeal8	Steps to Composition (Development of	1 copy	20	~~300~~ 240

	Writing Skill, Part-1)			
PujaDeal7	**Rhetoric & Prosody**	1 copy	20	~~240~~ 192
PujaDeal6	**Question Bank of English Grammar & Composition**	1 copy	20	~~559~~ 448
PujaDeal5	Study of Subject-Verb Agreement, Narration Change, Use of Punctuation; including Analysis, Synthesis & Split-up	1 copy	20	~~301~~ 241
PujaDeal4	Detail Study of Phrases, Clauses & Sentences, including Idioms & Phrasal Verbs	1 copy	20	~~290~~ 232
PujaDeal3	Study of Adverbs, Prepositions, Conjunctions & Interjections	1 copy	20	~~260~~ 208
PujaDeal2	All about Verbs (Forms, Functions, Conjugation, Tense, Voice Change, Forming Questions & Negation)	1 copy	18	~~420~~ 345
PujaDeal1	Study of Nouns, Pronouns, Adjectives & Articles (detail study)	1 copy	20	~~280~~ 224
unique01	**Peter's 'English Grammar'** (Complete Version of English Grammar)	1 copy	23	~~1201~~ 925
	FOR COPIES MORE THAN ONE			
bulk00	**Advanced Writing Skill, the Complete Version** (incl. Part-1, 2 & 3)	2 to 5000 copies	23	~~780~~ 601
Deal11	Development of Writing Skill, Part-3	2 to 5000 copies	24	~~365~~ 278
Deal10	Development of Writing Skill, Part-2	2 to 5000 copies	24	~~365~~ 278
Deal9	Steps to Composition (Development of Writing Skill, from Primary to Secondary Level)	2 to 5000 copies	26	~~300~~ 222
Deal8	**Rhetoric & Prosody**	2 to 5000 copies	26	~~240~~ 178
Deal7	**Question Bank of English Grammar & Composition**	2 to 5000 copies	28	~~559~~ 403
bulk01	**Peter's 'English Grammar'** (Complete Version of English Grammar)	2 to 5000 copies	30	~~1201~~ 841
Deal5	Study of Subject-Verb Agreement, Narration Change, Use of Punctuation; including Analysis, Synthesis & Split-up	2 to 5000 copies	26	~~301~~ 223
Deal4	Detail Study of Phrases, Clauses & Sentences, including Idioms & Phrasal Verbs	2 to 5000 copies	26	~~290~~ 215
Deal3	Study of Adverbs, Prepositions, Conjunctions & Interjections	2 to 5000 copies	26	~~260~~ 193
Deal2	All about Verbs (Forms, Functions, Conjugation, Tense, Voice Change, Forming Questions & Negation)	2 to 5000 copies	26	~~420~~ 311
Deal1	Study of Nouns, Pronouns, Adjectives & Articles (detail study)	2 to 5000 copies	26	~~280~~ 208

CONTENTS

Chapters pages

Outline of the book

The book deals in details of Phrases, Clauses and Sentences, as well as Moods or the Manner of Expression of verbs; and how, the classification of sentences is based upon 'Moods' and different clauses. It includes their definitions, comparisons to find out similarities and distinctions, as well as necessary examples in support of each point, given and discussed. The seven kinds of phrases, their type, nature and functions as well as the functions of their corresponding words (parts of speech) have been included and discussed through examples in sentences. It is shown, how clauses build simple, compound or complex sentences; besides, how to form affirmative, negative and interrogative sentences.

It is shown how mood, the form of verbs controls one way of classification of sentences (based on functions or uses), and how clauses define another way of classification of sentences (based on structure).

Different conditionals and wish clause have also been included and discussed. Different phrases (seven kinds) including a list of phrasal verbs as well as 372 idioms have also taken their share in this book of Mr. Peter.

1. Compare: Phrase, Clause & Sentence

1. **What is a Sentence?**

   A group of words, with a or more units of finite verbs, that makes a complete sense or expresses a complete thought, is called a Sentence; as,

   - Little Tom sways on the river.
   - He hardly could control his boat in the current of the river.
   - Sourabh turned to me.
   - What can we do to help you?
   - He is an aashiq.

Note: a unit of finite verb includes the main verb along with its all helping verbs in the sentence; as

- Peter ***has been working*** on this project since last year. (The three verbs together is considered to be one unit of finite verb.)
- Peter ***is working*** on a project which ***took*** more than eleven months. (***'is working'***—is considered as one unit of finite verb, whereas ***'took'*** is considered to be another unit of finite verb.)

2. **How to identify a sentence:**

A sentence generally begins with **a Capital Letter** & ends with a **Full Stop (.) or** a **Question (?) or** an **Exclamation Mark(!)**.

   - You don't know what you are talking about!
   - How many days will you take to say this?
   - You are a good girl.

3. **If the parts of a sentence** (i.e., the units of a language) **are arranged, according to their size, in ascending order, they are as—**

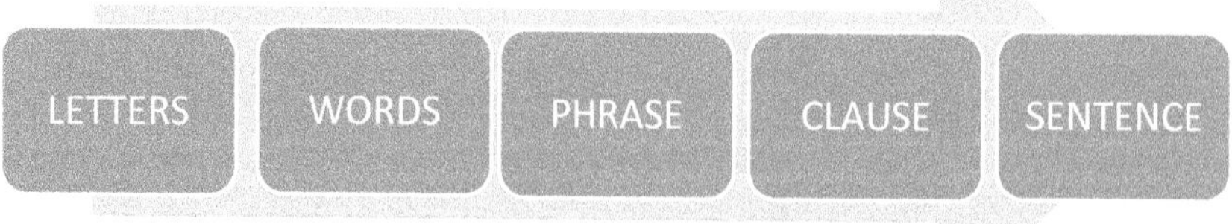

Letter → Word → Phrase → Clause, and → Sentence

Of the above, whereas, ***a word is the smallest unit of language,*** *(conveys a meaning);* ***a sentence is the standard unit of a language*** that conveys a complete thought of the speaker.

4. Let's compare them...

Letter (or, Alphabet)

- ***Letters are the special signs or symbols that build a word;***
- 26 letters (A to Z) in English are called together English alphabet.
- A letter neither forms a meaning nor a thought or a sense of the speaker.

Word

- A word is the smallest unit of language, forms a meaning;
- ***A group of letters or simply a letter while conveying a meaning is called a word.***

Phrase

- Two or more words together build a phrase or a clause or a sentence.
- Like a word, a *phrase is also a unit of language*, being a part of a sentence, but *larger than a word* and conveys an extended meaning.
- A phrase consists of a group of words, like a clause or a sentence.

5. **Read the Sentences:**
   - The sun rises ***in the east***.
   - Humpty Dumpty sat ***on a wall***.
   - There came a giant ***to my door***.
   - It was a sunset ***of great beauty***.
   - The tops ***of the mountains*** were covered with snow.
   - Show me ***how to do it***.

Note: *Examine the group of words, written in italics & bold.* What functions are they doing? Each group conveys a meaning of—*direction, position, movement, quality, possession* and *an action acted upon* (object) or *manner of action.*

All these are the examples of phrases in the sentences.

Let's discuss a bit more with explanation-

- The sun rises ***in the east***. (*in the east—refers to direction. It is made of a group of words and builds a meaning, broader one merely than 'east'. But it has no finite verb and does not form a complete thought. So, it is a phrase as a part of the sentence. As, it does the function of an Adverb, referring 'direction' only; so, it is an adverbial phrase.* In the chapter of Adverb and of phrase, you will get more such examples.)
- Humpty Dumpty sat ***on a wall***. (*on the wall—refers to position. It is an adverbial phrase of place.*)
- There came a giant ***to my door***. (*to my door— it is a phrase & adverb of movement.*)
- It was a sunset ***of great beauty***. (*of great beauty—meaning 'very beautiful—describing the scenic beauty of sunset. It is a phrase of Adjective.*)
- The tops ***of the mountains*** were covered ***with snow***. (*of the mountains—refers part or possession. The genitive case of Noun. So, it is the noun phrase. The other*, ***with snow*** *forms an object of a preposition. So, it is also a Noun Phrase.*)
- Show me ***how to do it***. (*Show me, what? How to do it—forms the object of the verb, 'show'. It is doing the function of a noun. So, it is a noun phrase, though begins with a relative or adjunctive adverb.* For identity depends on function rather than merely based on forms.)

6. Comparison—Phrase Vs Clause:

Phrase

- A phrase consists of a group of words.
- It has an extended meaning.
- It does not contain a subject & a finite verb.

Clause

- A clause, like a phrase, also consists of a group of words.
- It has a sense or a thought, complete or incomplete.
- It contains a subject & a finite verb.

7. Now, Read the following sentences:

- He has *a chain of gold*.
- He has a chain *which is made of gold*.

Note: Examine carefully the group of words, in italic & colour.

- We recognise the first group of words as ***a phrase***.

- The second group of words, unlike the phrase, *has something more than a phrase, like it* ***has a subject, 'which'*** *(a relative pronoun) and also a* ***finite verb*** *(i.e., predicate) 'is* ***made*** *of gold'*.
- The second group of words is called '***a clause***'.

8. Comparison—Clause Vs Sentence

Clause

- It is a part of a sentence, conveys a thought, complete or incomplete.
- A clause also is a unit of language.
- A clause, like a sentence, has a subject & a finite verb;
- In a clause there may have more phrases.

Sentence

- A sentence must have a complete sense or a thought of a person.
- A sentence is the largest & the standard grammatical or structural unit of language;
- A sentence must have a subject & a predicate.
- In a sentence there may have more phrases and clauses.

9. Remember:

Both a clause and a sentence have a subject and a predicate (i.e., finite verb). You have already read their differences too in the above.

In the following sentences, underline the clauses and circle the phrases & recall their differences:

1) People who pay their debts are trusted.
2) Banks trust the non-defaulter customers.
3) We cannot start while it is raining.
4) We can't start in the raining.
5) I think (that) you have made a history.
6) I am sure about your success.

Let's check your answer with the followings. Did they match all? If 'yes', congratulation! If you score 4 or less out of 6, you need further study them.

1) People ***who pay their debts*** are trusted.
2) Banks trust *the non-defaulter customers*.
3) We cannot start ***while it is raining***.
4) We can't start *in the raining*.
5) I think (that) ***you have made a history***.

6) I am sure *about your success.*

- From 1 to 6—all are the sentences, for each one conveys a complete thought or idea of the speaker.
- In 1), 3) & 5)—there is more than one finite verb in each sentence. Thus, each one has two clauses. **The bold italic are the subordinate clauses,** while the italic-colored words are the example of phrases.

10. Kinds of Sentences:

Sentences are of five kinds, according to the functions or their mode of expression, and these are:

(1) **Assertive Sentence** or Statement:
(2) **Interrogative Sentence** or Question:
(3) **Imperative Sentence** or the Sentence of Order, Request or Advice:
(4) **Optative Sentence** or the Sentence of Suggest, Prayer or Wish:
(5) **Exclamatory Sentence** or the Sentence of feelings or emotion:

Note: Remember, there is another division of sentences, and that is based on their formation or structure. Details are in the chapter of Sentence.

11. Definitions of Sentences, based on functions & their examples:

- **Assertive Sentence** or **Statement**: An Assertive sentence is also called a **Declarative Sentence**. They make a statement or declare something; as,
  - Humpty Dumpty sat on a wall.
  - Maa looked at me.
- **Interrogative Sentence** or **Question**: A sentence that asks questions; as,
  - Where do you live? What do you like?
  - Do you want it? What's your name?
- **Imperative Sentence** or the **Sentence of Order, Request or Advice**: A sentence which expresses commands, requests, entreaties; as,
  - Get out from here. Get lost from my life.

- You should do it. Please give me a glass of water.

- **Optative Sentence** or the **Sentence of Suggest, Prayer or Wish**: A sentence that express wish, prayer or suggest; as,
    - May God bless you, my child.
    - If I were a bird. Let's play football.

- **Exclamatory Sentence** or the **Sentence of feelings or emotion**: A sentence that expresses strong feelings; as,
    - What a shame! the dean of the college?
    - Look, how lovely the hill!

2. Detail study: 7 kinds of Phrases

12. A phrase is a unit of language, smaller than a clause and a sentence, and larger than a word. A phrase may be a part of a clause as well as of a sentence, but not the reverse. **Like a sentence and a clause**, a phrase also consists of a group of words, but it does not have any finite verb like the clause or a sentence.
A phrase builds a meaning block, like a word, but not a sense or thought like a sentence.

The classification of phrase depends on the nature of different words and their functions. Or in other words, it can be said, **a phrase does function like words (seven parts of speech, except 'pronoun'**), and are named accordingly; like,

1) Noun or Nominal Phrase,
2) Adjective or Relative Phrase,
3) Phrasal Verbs,
4) Adverbial Phrase,
5) Prepositional Phrase,
6) Conjunctive phrase, and the
7) Phrase of Interjection.

- ❑ And, we have not any Pronoun Phrase

13. **The Definition of a Phrase:** **When a group of words,** without a subject & a finite verb, **form a meaning**, like a word, in the sentence, is called a Phrase.

14. **The Noun or Nominal Phrase:** That does the work of a Noun. Study the following sentences:

- It is uncertain.
- **My going home** is uncertain.
- The boy wants something.
- The boy wants **to go home**.

In sentence 1, the word **'it'** is a pronoun and it is the subject of the verb. Similarly, the group of words ***'my going home'*** in sentence 2 is the subject of the verb 'is'.

In sentence 3, the word ***'something'*** is the object of the verb 'wants. And similarly, the group of words in sentence 4 ***'to go home'*** is the object of the verb 'wants.

Thus, in each case, *the word* or *the group of words* do the function of a Noun. So, the group of words, which is a phrase, is known as **'Noun Phrase'**, doing the function of a Noun.

For more examples, read the following sentences:

1) He likes to play football
2) He enjoys walking by the river side.
3) He enjoys walking in the morning.
4) Akbar, the Mughal emperor, conquered.
5) We made him the captain of the class.
6) Early to bed is a good maxim.
7) We enjoy playing cricket.
8) Did you enjoy reading this book?
9) To win a prize is my ambition.
10) He hopes to win the first prize.
11) He loves to issue harsh orders.
12) I tried to get the sum right.
13) Standing about in a cold wet wind did me no good.

In above, all the underlined have done the work of a Noun, so they are the **Noun Phrases** in the sentences.

15. Exercise-1: Pick out Noun Phrases from the following sentences:

1) His father wished to speak to the Head master.
2) He dislikes having to punish his servants.
3) Horses prefer living in dark stables.
4) Is should hate to do such a thing.
5) Have you ever tried climbing a coconut palm?
6) Thinking good thoughts precedes good actions.
7) He refuses to answer the questions.
8) Promise to come again.
9) Why do you like visiting such a man?
10) Travelling in a hot dusty train gives me no pleasure.
11) He denies stealing the money.
12) You're doing such a thing (that) surprises me.

You may check your answers with the followings.

answers

1) His father wished to speak to the Head master.
2) He dislikes having to punish his servants.
3) Horses prefer living in dark stables.
4) I should hate to do such a thing.
5) Have you ever tried climbing a coconut palm?
6) Thinking good thoughts precedes good actions.
7) He refuses to answer the questions.
8) Promise to come again.
9) Why do you like visiting such a man?
10) Travelling in a hot dusty train gives me no pleasure.
11) He denies stealing the money.
12) You're doing such a thing (that) surprises me.

16. The Adjective or Relative Phrase: That does the work of an Adjective. Study the following sentences:

1) He gave me a chain *of gold*. (= a **gold** chain)
2) My friend is *without fear*. (=**fearless**)
3) I am *free from blame*. (=**blameless**)
4) It is a deed *of a hero*. (a **heroic** deed)
5) He is a man *of fame*. (=**famous** man)
6) This is a cycle *made in England*. (**English** cycle/ *English made* cycle)

- Within bracket the bold word is the single form of Adjective phrase written in italic. In each case, the phrase does a work of an Adjective; they each have described certain Nouns.

- **Now study the following pair of sentences carefully:**

1) Tata was a *wealthy* man.
    - Tata was a man ***of great wealth***.
2) The magistrate was a *kind* man.
    - The magistrate was a man ***of kindly nature***.
3) The chief lived in a *stone* house.
    - The chief lived in a house ***built of stone***.
4) I like to see a *smiling* face.
    - I like to see a face ***with a smile on it***.
5) The coolies belonged to a *hill* tribe.

- The coolies belonged to a tribe ***dwelling in the hills***.

6) The king wears a *golden* crown.
   - The kings wear a crown ***made of gold***.

- Study the table relating **Adjectives & their corresponding Adjective Phrases:**

Adjective	***Adjective Phrase***
1) A purple clock	1) A cloak of purple color.
2) A white elephant	2) An elephant with white skin.
3) A jungle tracks	3) A track through the jungle.
4) A blue-eyed boy	4) A boy with blue eyes.
5) A deserted village	5) A village without any inhabitants.
6) A blank page	6) A page with no writing on it.
7) The longest day	7) The day of greatest length.
8) The Spanish flag	8) The flag of Spain.
9) A heavy load	9) A load of great weight.
10) He is **well**.	10) He is **fit & fine/healthy & sound**.
11) A **valuable** ring was found yesterday.	11) A ring **of worthy** was found yesterday.
12) **Heroic** deeds deserve our admiration.	12) Deeds **of a hero** deserve our admiration.
13) Much has been said about the **Swiss** scenery.	13) Much has been said about the scenery **of Switzerland.**
14) The Rajputs were passionately fond of **martial** glory.	14) The Rajputs were passionately fond of glory **of war**.
15) **Numerical** superiority is a great advantage.	15) The superiority **of numbers** is a great advantage.
16) I have passed two **sleepless** nights.	16) I have passed two nights **of sleepless**.
17) He is a **professional** cricketer.	17) He is a cricketer **by profession**.
18) This book contains many **biblical** quotations.	18) This book contains many quotations **of Bible**.
19) She wants **medical** advice.	19) She wants advice **of medical expert**.
20) A **tall** soldier stepped forth.	20) A soldier **of high length** stepped forth.
21) He is a **friendless** man.	

	21) He is a man *without a friend*.
22) They came to a **muddy** path.	22) They came to a path *covered with mud*.
23) He carried a **blood-stained** sword.	23) He carried a sword *stained with blood*.
24) I met a little **cottage** girl.	24) I met a little girl *from a cottage*.
25) Balu was a highly **impudent** person.	25) Balu was a man *with plenty of impudence*.
26) From this **mountain**-village came the army chief at present.	26) From this village *in the mountains* came the army chief at present.
27) The Rajput leader was a **hopeful fearless** soldier.	27) The Rajput leader was a soldier *full of hope and free from fear*.
28) Nelson was a **fearless** boy.	28) Nelson was a boy *without a fear*.
29) Nobody likes a **bad-tempered** person.	29) Nobody likes a person *with a bad temper*.
30) I admit that he is a **sensible** man.	30) I admit that he is a man *of sense*.
31) The **mountain** tops were covered with snow.	31) The tops *of the mountains* were covered with snow.
32) He is a **versatile** author.	32) He is an author *of great versatility*.
33) It is **useless**.	33) It is *of no use*.

- **To be noted:** Though we may replace many adjectives with the adjective or relative phrases, all adjective phrases cannot be replaced by single Adjectives & vice-versa or that may not suit to the sense of the sentence always; as the followings:
  1) The man ***in the street*** knows it. (We can't write: 'The street man knows it', because that may refer or denote a different meaning from the actual sense.)
  2) The tree ***in front of my house*** has been cut down. (Similarly, we can't write: 'The front tree'. And the same thing happens for the following phrases too.)
  3) A boy ***desirous of winning the prize*** must work hard.
  4) He never felt the witchery ***of the soft blue sky***.
  5) In a low voice he told the tale ***of his cruel wrongs***.

6) The police arrested a man ***of one of the criminal tribes***.
7) A man ***in great difficulties*** came to me for help.
8) Wild beasts ***in small cages*** are a sorry sight.
9) A man ***without an enemy*** is a man with few friends.

17. The Comparative study of Noun & Adjective phrases side by side. Remember, the phrase, **Adjective or Noun**, depends on the **work they do** in the sentence & extension of meaning. Study the table.

As a Noun Phrase	As an Adj. or Relative Phrase
1) He enjoys walking by the river-side.	1) The boy ***walking by the river-side*** is my brother.
2) I gave the book to the desirous of winning the prize.	2) A boy ***desirous of winning the prize*** must work hard.
3) A turban made of silk is worthy for him.	3) He wore a turban ***made of silk***.
4) He has done a shameful deed.	4) He has done a deed ***of shame.***
5) He led a blameless life.	5) He led a life ***devoid of blame***.

18. Exercise-1: **Italicize Adjective Phrases in the following sentences:**

a) A man in great difficulties came to me for help.
b) He is a person of very considerable renown.
c) Wild beasts in small cages are a sorry sight.
d) A man without an enemy is a man with few friends.
e) He tells a tale with the ring of truth in it.
f) A friend in need is a friend indeed.
g) A stitch in time saves nine.
h) A bird in hand is worth two in the bush.
i) Gardens with cool shady trees surround the village.
j) Only a man with plenty of money buys a car of such luxuries in it.
k) In a low voice he told the tale of his cruel wrongs.
l) Do you know the story of the noble Padmini?
m) He was a lad of great promise.
n) He bore a banner with strange device.

Answer of Exercise-1

a) A man ***in great difficulties*** came to me for help.
b) He is a person ***of very considerable renown***.

c) Wild beasts ***in small cages*** are a sorry sight.
d) A man ***without an enemy*** is a man with few friends.
e) He tells a tale ***with the ring of truth*** in it.
f) A friend ***in need*** is a friend indeed.
g) A stitch ***in time*** saves nine.
h) A bird ***in hand*** is worth two ***in the bush***.
i) Gardens ***with cool shady trees*** surround the village.
j) Only a man ***with plenty of money*** buys a car ***of such luxuries*** in it.
k) In a low voice he told the tale ***of his cruel wrongs***.
l) Do you know the story ***of the noble Padmini***?
m) He was a lad ***of great promise***.
n) He bore a banner ***with strange device***.

19. Exercise-2: **Replace the Adjectives in bold by an Adjective Phrase of the same meaning**:

a) A **grey** cloud spread over the sky.
b) He dwelt in a **wooden** hut.
c) He had a **bald** head.
d) She wore a **diamond** necklace.
e) It was a **horrible** night.
f) They went by **Siberian** railway.
g) A **grassy** meadow stretched before us.
h) An **earthen** pitcher stood on a **three-legged** table.
i) The **French** flag flew at the top of the **highest** mast.
j) That was a **cowardly** act.

answers

a) A cloud **grey in color** spread over the sky.
b) He dwelt in a hut **made of wood**.
c) He had headed **with bald**.
d) She wore a necklace **made of diamond.**
e) It was a night **full of horrible sight**.
f) They went by railway **that runs through Siberia**. (It is a clause)
g) A meadow **full of grass** stretched before us.
h) A pitcher **made of earth** stood on a table **of three legs**.
i) The flag **of France** flew at the top of the mast **of highest height**.
j) That was an act **of a coward**.

Compare Phrasal Verbs & Idioms

20. The Phrasal Verbs or Group Verbs: A main verb often takes helping or auxiliary verbs in tenses and voice change. This is a normal structure of finite verbs to build a meaning; and in this case, the main verb always dominates the auxiliary or helping verbs to form meaning of the sentence, and even with different auxiliary verbs, the main meaning remains intact, except 'time of an action or state'; as,

- He **is going** to Kolkata.
- He **has been reading** the novel for two hours.
- I **shall have been** there by the time.
- The mango **is eaten** by me.
- He **does not eat** fruits.

The above is the normal usage of verbs along with their helping or auxiliary verbs, as per tense in active or passive voice. They are each a unit of finite verb to form tense or voice change.

But sometimes, the main verb is used with other parts of speech, mainly preposition or an adverb and often with both *forms a special or unique meaning, which is different from the* individual words (they are formed or built of), are called the **Phrasal** or **Group verbs**.

Definition: When ***a verb with a preposition*** or ***an adverb*** or ***both*** builds a completely new meaning is called a Phrasal or Group Verb.

The group verbs are called Phrasal Verbs because they are in the form of a phrase and have a particular meaning from the words they are built of.

Study the following for better understand:

- **Get:** to receive something (verb)
- **By:** the method of doing something (preposition)
- **Get by:** live with difficulty

Did you notice how the words ***'get'*** and ***'by'*** have different meanings when they are used individually than when they are used together?

When the two words are used together, they form a phrasal verb ***'get by'***.

Read another example:

- He ***gives*** me all that I need.
- ***Give up*** your bad habit.

In the first sentence, the verb has its general meaning, here to mean 'providing something'. Even we add helping verb with it; like, **'He will give me all that I need'** the main meaning 'providing something' remains intact, only the tense (time of action) is changed. But:

In the second sentence, the verb **'give'** with the preposition **'up'** builds a different meaning from the words *'give'* and *'up'* ('up' to mean above position). Here the group verb **'give up'** *has unique meaning* to mean **'abandon'**.

Thus, a particular verb with different prepositions and adverbial particles ***expresses different meanings*** and also different, in general, from the words they are built of.

Study, how the phrasal verbs different in meanings from words they are made of:

Verb	**Meaning**	**Phrasal Verbs**	**Meaning**
Bring	Come carrying something	Bring up	Rear somebody
Call	Ask someone to come	Call on	Visit somewhere
Get	Receive	Get up	Awake
Look	See	Look into	Investigate
Make	Prepare	Make out	Comprehend
Put	Keep something	Put on	Wear
Take	Carry something	Take after	Resemble /look like

- I shall ***call on*** him tomorrow. (I shall ***visit*** him tomorrow)

- She ***brought up*** her child to be a kind man, a term full of confusion.
- I ***get up*** early every day.
- Please sir, ***look into*** the matter. He made us homeless.
- Do you ***make out*** the difference between a verb and a phrasal verb?
- ***Put on*** your unform, it is time to move on.
- The girl ***takes after*** her mother.

Some of Phrasal Verbs for their universal use & significance in expressions are also termed as ***Idioms***.

However, the term ***'idioms*** 'refer to all kinds of phrases that includes *prepositional*, *nominal*, *relative*, certain *phrasal verbs* & also *adverbial* which are **significant and very popular in meaning since long past to be used by people**.

However, please study the chapters of '**Idioms**' for more details & examples.
And for more **Phrasal Verbs** to know in details and examples, please go through the next chapters of '**List of Phrasal Verbs**'.

21. **The Adverbial Phrase:** That does the work of an Adverb.

1) He was ***at that place*** (there). The arrow fell ***on this spot*** (here).
2) Goutam babu does his work ***with care***. (Carefully).
3) The thief fled/ran away ***at a great speed***. (fast/quickly).
4) Come ***before long/ at an early date*** (soon).
5) The coins from the bag scattered ***in all places*** (everywhere).
6) He answered ***in a rude manner*** (rudely).
7) He fell ***to the ground*** (down).
8) He does his work ***without any care*** (carelessly).
9) I have no money ***at this moment*** (now).
10) No such diseases were known ***in those days*** (then).

❑ More about Adverbial Phrases:

11) He came to *see me*. (purpose/reason)

12) He fell *from the tree*. (direction)
13) Come *into the garden*. (adv. of place)
14) This must be done at *any cost*. (manner)
15) He lives *on a small income*. (manner)
16) Quinine is good *for malaria*. (purpose/ causes)
17) I have done well *on the whole*. (manner)
18) He swims *in the pond*. (where-place)
19) She lived *in the middle of a great wood*. (place)
20) I stood *on the bridge at midnight*. (place & time)
21) I took him *on the strength of your recommendation*. (Why-reason)

- Some more adverbial phrases, try them to use in your sentences:

Adverbial Phrases	Adverbial Phrases
1) In a loud voice	11) On either side of the street.
2) Without further delay	12) In a shady nook
3) With one voice	13) To the last man
4) For certain	14) With a smile
5) Just in time	15) At sixes and sevens
6) Up in arms	16) At the eleventh hour
7) Of no consequence	17) On the top of the hill
8) Out of fashion	18) In future
9) With great satisfaction	19) At nine o'clock
10) In the twinkling of an eye.	20) With great promptitude.

- Like relative phrases many can be replaced by single adverb or word, but not all. However, see the chart, which can be replaced like in the following:

Adverbs	Adverbial Phrases

1) Bravely	1) In a brave manner/ with bravery
2) Unwisely	2) In an unwise manner/ without wisdom
3) Swiftly	3) In a swift manner/ with swiftness
4) Beautifully	4) In a beautiful style
5) Formerly	5) In former times / once upon a time
6) Recently	6) Just now / at a recent date
7) Soon	7) Before very long/ at an early date.
8) Here	8) At this place
9) There	9) At that place
10) Away	10) To another place
11) Abroad	11) To or in a foreign country
12) Now	12) At this moment
13) Then	13) In those days, etc.

❑ Besides, there are many phrases which can be used as *both as Adjective and* as *Adverb*. Study the chart.

As an Adjective Phrase	*As an Adverbial Phrase*
1) The man in the room rushed out.	1) He is in the room.
2) The work at night I don't like.	2) Knock me at night.
3) The man sleeps at noon, doesn't mean idle.	3) They went there at noon.
4) The crowd in the bazaar was very noisy.	4) The crowd halted in the bazaar.
5) Have you heard of the man in the moon?	5) How could be a man in the moon?
6) A house on an island was washed away.	6) They live on an island.
7) Awful is the gloom beneath her.	7) Then why did she look beneath her?
8) Is this the train to Peshawar?	8) It usually goes to Peshawar, Sir.

22. Exercise-1: Replace the Adverb Phrases by an Adverb of same meaning:

1) The bodies were mangled **in a terrible manner.**
2) Let us cease work **from this very moment**.
3) It was just **on this spot**

9) I accept your statement **without reserve.**
10) I thank you with **all my heart**.
11) He succeeded **in the**

that he died.

4) The child replied **with perfect truthfulness**.
5) He arrived at that moment.
6) I hope that he will come **at a very early date.**
7) He seems to have acted **with great promptitude.**
8) No one would dare to answer him **in an impudent way.**

long run.

12) He is ignorant **to a proverb**.
13) The post-boy drove **with fierce career.**
14) He has been painted **in his proper colors.**
15) The wind blew **with great violence.**
16) He has proved his case **to my satisfaction.**

23. Exercise-2: Replace the Adverb in italics by an Adverb phrase of same meaning:

1) The pigeon flies **swiftly**.
2) Did Rama behave **well**?
3) Go **away**.
4) The dying man replied **feebly**.
5) **Gently** fell the rain.
6) We will pitch the tents just **here**.
7) He expects to get promotion **soon**.
8) He builds his house **there**.
9) He tried **hard**.
10) They have only **recently** arrived.
11) Al though hungry, the soldiers worked **cheerfully**.
12) He spoke **eloquently**.
13) **Soon** the sun will set.
14) Do you work **thoroughly**?
15) They were hurrying **homeward**.
16) The door was **suspiciously** open.
17) **Formerly** he worked at the School of Economics.

24. The Prepositional Phrase:

In the chapter of Preposition, we have discussed 6 kinds of Prepositions. Of them the number 4 is about the Prepositional Phrase. Read the definition and study the examples.

- He stood *in front of* me.
- I was *at the point of* death.
- *In the teeth of* strong opposition, the bill was passed.
- *On account of* his illness, he failed in the Exam.

- In most cases the *prepositions do the function of an Adverb*, i.e., they are adverbial in nature; as in '***in front of***' denotes the position of verb, 'where did he stand?'

- The Prepositions which are formed by two or more words, with the force of a single preposition at the end, is called the **Prepositional Phrase** or **Complex Preposition**; as, *according to, because of, as for owing to, due to,* etc.

- Here is a list of Prepositional Phrase which is actually drawn from the chapter of Prepositions. Study them, if done already, here as a revision:

1) Act ***according to*** my instructions. Why don't you come ***along with*** us?
2) **Agreeably to** the terms of the settlement, I herewith enclose my cheque for Rs 20000.
3) He could not attend the classes ***because of*** his illness.
4) ***By reason of*** his perverse attitude, he estranged his best friends.
5) ***In consequence of*** his illness, he could not finish the work in time.
6) ***In event of*** his dying heirless, his nephew would inherit the whole property.
7) There is an open field ***in front of*** our house. He got the flat ***in lieu of*** all his sundry.
8) I took Arts ***in place of*** science. ***In spite of*** hard labor, he could not succeed.
9) Mrs. Gosh joined the meeting ***instead of*** her husband. He went there ***instead of*** me.
10) ***Owing to*** excessive rain, the flood occurs this year.
11) Rs 75,000 ***in full settlement of*** all your claims up-to-date.
12) Whatever he does, he does ***with an eye to*** the main chance.
    - **Exception:** Some phrases do not take any simple preposition at end; as, '***on this side***', '***on board***', etc.
13) ***On this side*** you can see the stretched green land.
14) ***On board***, she recalled her boyfriend & rushed towards the door.

- **Check the list of Complex Preposition or Prepositional Phrase:**

Prepositional Phrases	Meaning...	Examples

At home in	Familiar with/skilled in	He is quite at home in Mathematics.
At the top of	Highest point	The man began to cry at the top of his cry.
Because of	Due to reason	She could not sing because of cough & cold.
By dint of	With help	By dint of hard work, he succeeded.
By force of	By power of	Even a difficult thing is made easy by force of habit.
By means of	Way of/virtue of	He won the honor by means of selfless service.
By the side of	Beside	A small river flows by the side of the small village.
By virtue of	With help	She stood first by virtue of hard labor.
For the sake of	For/cause	Netaji sacrificed his life for the sake of his country.
For want of	Due to lack of	The drought occurs for want of rain.
In accordance with	accordingly,	Your action is not in accordance with your word.
In connection with	Relating	In connection with your query, I am writing this letter.

In case of	If happen (something)	In case of his death his son will get the benefit.
Prepositional Phrases	*Meaning...*	*Examples*
In common with	Agree with	You should also be favored with the others.
In course of	During the time	In course of conversation, he also mentioned it.
In consideration of	Considering	In consideration of his hard work, he may succeed.
In defense of	In support of	The pleader made a good proceeding in defense of his client.
In favor of	In support of	The students spoke in support of their teacher.
In front of	Before/at front	They saw a hut in front of the palace.
In keeping with	Accordance with	His interest in religion is in keeping with his age.
In lieu of	Instead of/in place of	Please take my subscription in lieu of her.
In opposition to	On contrary of	Your view is in opposition to mine.
In order to	For/ due to	In order to get a good result, he studied very hard.
In quest of	For seek of	He went to the town in quest of any job.

In regard to	Regarding/about	I have nothing to say in regard to this matter.
In reply/response to	Giving reply	In response to your advertisement, I am writing this.
Prepositional Phrases	*Meaning...*	*Examples*
In respect of	Regarding	In respect of service, he is senior to me.
In spite of	Even of	In spite of his poverty, he refused help.
In support of	In support of	The students spoke in support of their teacher.
In the teeth of	Against	In the teeth of strong opposition, the bill was passed.
In view of	On considering	In view of the importance, I'll take prime carefulness.
On account of	Because of/due to	On account of his illness, he failed in the Exam.
On behalf of	For (somebody)	On behalf of me kindly give it to my wife.
On the brink of	At the point of	Bengal was on the brink of a terrible famine in 1942.

On the eve of	At the moment	He made a great confusion on the eve of the occasion.
On the point of	At the moment of	She was on the point of bursting into tears.
With a view to	For purpose of	He went to Delhi with a view to taking part...
With reference to	Referring/mentioning	With reference to your letter, I have the honor to inform you.

25. The Conjunctional or **Conjunctive Phrase:** The conjunctions that consist of two or more words, they are called the **conjunctional phrases**; as, *as well as, inasmuch as, as soon as, in order that, even if, as if,* etc.
The Correlative (that are used in pair; as, *either—or, neither—nor, though—yet,* etc.) & Compound Conjunctions (that are used with two or more words, i.e., *as well as, inasmuch as, as soon as, in order that, even if, as if,* etc.) –are the examples of **Conjunctional Phrases**; as, [for more details about the classification of Conjunctions, please read the chapter of Conjunctions.]

1) He walks ***as though*** he is slightly lame.
2) I must refuse your request, ***inasmuch as*** I believe it unreasonable.
3) He took off his coat ***as soon as*** he entered the house.
4) He looks ***as if*** he were weary.

❑ **Study them some more in details:**

The Correlative Conjunctions are again classified into — *Cumulative*, *Alternative* & *Adversative* in nature. They are like the followings:

A. **Cumulative Correlative**: (both—and, not only—but also)
- We ***both*** love ***and*** honor him.
- ***Not only*** is he foolish, ***but also*** obstinate.

B. **Alternative Correlative**: (Either...or, neither...nor, whether—or)
- ***Either*** take it ***or*** leave it.
- It is ***neither*** useful ***nor*** ornamental.

- ***Whether*** he'll go ***or*** I have to.
- I do not care ***whether*** you go ***or*** stay.

C. **Adversative Correlative**: (though—yet,)

- ***Though*** he is suffering much pain, ***yet*** he does not complain.
- ***Though*** he worked hard, ***yet*** he failed in the test.

❑ **And, more examples of Compound Conjunctions** which also belong to the Conjunctional Phrase (a phrase which consists of two or more words). ***Remember,*** *the Compound Conjunctions in form or structure may also be either of both, Sub-ordinate Conjunction or Co-ordinate Conjunction regarding the function.*

- The notice was published ***in order that*** all might know the facts.
- I will forgive you ***on condition that*** you do not repeat the offence.
- Such an act would not be kind ***even if*** it were just.
- He saved some bread ***so that*** he should not go hungry on the morrow.
- You can borrow the book ***provided that*** you return it soon.
- I must refuse your request, ***inasmuch as*** I believe it unreasonable.
- He took off his coat ***as soon as*** he entered the house.
- He looks ***as if*** he were weary.

❑ All the above are also the **Sub-Ordinate Conjunctions** *(regarding functions)*; besides they are the examples of **Compound Conjunctions** *(regarding structure).*

❑ But, as we said, a **Compound Conjunction** may also be a **Co-Ordinate Conjunction** like the following, and they all belong to the **conjunctive phrase**:

- Prakash ***as well as*** Pravat were absent from school.
- ***Both*** Prakash ***and*** Pravat were absent from the school.

26. The Interjectional Phrase:

Like Pronoun, Interjection has almost no* Phrases, or have few to mention. Many grammarians wish to exclude even, the interjection to be a part of the 'Parts of Speech'. However, as they have not given any different name (substitute term for interjection), we like continue to honor it as one of the 'Parts of Speech' as the other seven.

Note-1: * = The word of negation 'no' (an adjective) can be used with both singular & plural following it.

'Interjection has **almost no** Phrases'; it means it has 'few' or 'some phrases though'. It does not mean 'zero'.

To realize the **Phrase of Interjection**, please study the following pages (copied from the chapter of Interjections.) They are like the following:

- ✓ **What a pity!** he drowned!
- ✓ **By Jove!** we have got it.
- ✓ **Good heavens!** Protect us from this danger to grab.

❑ ***Definition:*** When two or more words together express an emotion is called a **Phrase of Interjection.**

Certain Phrases used as Interjections

There are certain phrases which are also used as the interjections in the sentences. Carefully study the sentences:

1) **Ah me!** You hate your life long.
2) **Well done friend!** You have done excellent.
3) **Good bye!** We don't know will we meet again?
4) **O dear me!** What you have done.
5) **Bad luck to it!** He tried his best yet.
6) **Good gracious!** How one can do this alone.
7) **Good heavens!** Who can do it?
8) **Well, to be sure!** It is he has done this job.
9) **For shame!** Leave me alone.
10) **Alas & alack!** We had missed our bus.

Certain Verbs or other Parts of Speech, used as Interjections too

There are *certain moods of verbs* or *parts of speech* that are used as the interjections in the sentences:

a. Imperative:

→ **Hear!** What a song she sings.
→ **Hear! Hear!** What a sound it is. (*applause*)
→ **See!** What the sight is.

b. Subjunctive:

→ *Would that I had* the wings of a dove!
→ *Would that I had* billions of dollars!
→ *Would that I had* that great soul of Jesus!
(Thus, the whole sentence in subjunctive mood used in expressing wish of the speaker)

c. By infinitive:

→ **To think** that I should have played the match!
→ **To say** that I should go there! Why you not then?

d. Adjective or Adverb:

→ **Strange!** She went there.
→ **Shocking!** How she can say so.

Note: *Think:* strange or shocking—what? Or who? Is it 'she' or 'her going there' or 'saying that'? Are the words adjectives or adverbs? However, here in the above sentences the words are used as Interjections that expresses emotion of the speaker.

e. Adjective+ Noun:

→ **Dreadful sight!** I can't explain.
→ **Foolish fellow!** Or how one can behave before sure death.
→ **What a mess!** Who did all these!

f. Adverb:

→ **How** vary kind of you! If you didn't do, I fell in ...
→ **How** wonderful! **How** beautiful! How awful it is.

g. A full sentence with a pronoun:

→ What a sad thing **it** is! She died in shock of her husband's death.

h. A full sentence with a conjunction:

→ **If** I could see her once more! But I know it is now an improbable word to hope for her any longer.

'Wh' word sometimes with main verb, used also as Interjections

Sometimes while expressing strong emotion in hasty, Auxiliary verb with Subject is left out, and only main verb is used, with a 'wh' word; as,

- **Reached!** When?
- **Murdered!** How?
- **Why cry!** And for the man who has already forgotten you?
- **Why wait and spoil life!** Waiting for nothing come readymade.
- **Why go there!** You didn't tell it before.
- **What said!** I can't remember like that anything.
- **How reached!** And alone!
- **Wow!** But where it happened. /**Where happened!**

Note: Thus, we can express interjections in various ways than till mentioned, for interjections are not only words but it includes sounds various to count, i.e., unending, I meant to say.

3. The list of Phrasal Verbs

27. We said, Group or Phrasal Verbs are formed by combining **Verbs** and **Adverbs** or **Prepositions** or **both.** Let's check in the following:

A. Verb + Adverb = Phrasal Verbs

Verb	*Adverb*	***Phrasal Verbs***	***Meanings***
Bear	Down	Bear down	He was determined to bear down all obstacles. (to defeat)
Break	Away	Break away	The prisoner broke away from captivity. (escaped suddenly)
Bring	Out	Bring out	My first novel was brought out in 2020 during lockdown. (published)
Call	Out	Call out	He was called out for an urgent task. (summoned)
Go	Up	Go up	The price of essential commodities is going up. (increasing)
Set	Down	Set down	The police set down the complaint. (recorded)
Run	Over	Run over	A poor dog was run over by the car.
Turn	Aside	Turn aside	We should not turn aside from the path of

			honesty.

B. Verb + Prepositions = Phrasal Verbs

Verb	*Preposition*	***Phrasal Verbs***	***Meanings***
Bring	On	Bring on	The damp weather has brought on his illness. (led to)
Call	At	Call at	We called him at his house. (met)
Carry	On	Carry on	I am carrying on the project of publishing my academic books since 2021. (continuing)
Laugh	At	Laugh at	Your friends may laugh at you. Still, you move on. (mock at/show negligence)
Look	After	Look after	Parents look after their children to their utmost end. (take care of)
Put	On	Put on	You don't need put on you are an honest man. (take disguise)
Run	At	Run at	The tiger ran at the deer. (chased)
Set	Up	Set up	I set up my White Home by June, 2020. (founded)

C. Verb + Adverb + Prepositions = Phrasal Verbs

Verb	*Adverb*	*Prepositions*	***Phrasal Verbs***	***Meanings***
Look	Down	Upon	Look down upon	We should not look down upon the poor. (hate)
Set	Out + for	-	Set out for	They set out for the picnic spot early in the morning. (started)
Do	Away	With	Do away with	The young actress tried to do away with herself. (kill/try to commit suicide)
Fall	--	In + with	Fall in with	The Principal fell in with the decision of the guardian committee. (agree/give consent)

28. Study the following Phrasal Verbs used in sentences, arranged alphabetically: It begins with 'A':

A for 'Act', 'Aim at'

Group Verbs	Examples	Meanings
Act against	We should not act against other's opinion in general.	Do anything against
Act for	He is acting for his client.	Working on behalf of
Act on	He acted on my advice. So, his failure is my responsibility.	Worked according to
Act upon (1)	The medicine acts upon the heart.	affects
Act upon (2)	They acted upon our instructions.	Did as per
Act upon (3)	Acting upon the news, I went there.	Based upon/ depending on
Act up to	The machine does not act up to my expectation.	Work according to
Aim at	Riya aims at nothing.	(Wish target or goal)

B *for* **'Bear', 'Blow' 'Break', 'Bring', 'Burst'**

Group Verbs	Examples	Meanings
Back up	He **backed up** his friend's claim.	(supported)
Bear away	Preston bore away the prize for his talent.	Won
Bear down	He is determined to bear down all obstacles.	To defeat/ overcome
Bear on	These are the issues that bear on the welfare of the society.	Relate to
Bear out	The report bears out the accusation to be true. Dr. Roy will bear me out what I'll say.	Supports/ confirms
Bear up	The soldiers bore up their courage against all odds.	Kept up/ sustained
Bear with	I have to bear with her patiently during this difficult period.	tolerate
	Blow	
Blow away	The wind blew away all dry leaves.	Drove away
Blow in/into	The door opened and the school boys blew into the class rooms.	Arrive noisily,

		cheerfully
Blow off	The chimneys blow off thick smoke.	Emit
Blow out	Don't blow out the fire. We need it later.	Extinguish /put out
Blow over	• The storm soon will blow over and weather would be fine and pleasant. • The present disturbances will soon **blow over**.	(Pass off)
Blow up (1)	Opponent soldiers **blew up** the buildings.	(exploded)
Blow up (2)	A storm is blowing up.	Blowing fiercely
Blow up (3)	You don't need to blow up your credits.	Exaggerate
	Break	
Break away	The prisoner broke away from captivity. The accused broke away from the lock-up	Escaped suddenly/ freed himself
Break down (1)	His health broke down under the pressure of work.	Grew worse
Break down (2)	He **broke down** in the middle of his speech.	(failed) collapsed
Break forth	The sun broke forth from the clouds, and Arjuna killed Joydrowth.	Suddenly came out/ appeared
Break in /into (1)	The robbers broke in at night and took away all with them.	Forced their way in
Break in (2)	The horses are being broken in.	Trained
Break in (3)	He **broke in** our serious discussion and asked for a glass of water.	(interrupted)
Break into	Dacoits broke into the building last night.	Entered by force
Break in upon	The mob broke in upon the meeting and submitted their petition.	Made their way in by force

Break off (1)	He broke off in the middle of his speech.	Stopped speaking
Break off (2)	Sophia broke off her engagement with Fellix.	separated
Break out (1)	A devastating fire broke out due to short circuit.	Started suddenly
Break out (2)	Several prisoners broke out from jail.	Escaped by breaking.
Break through (1)	Scientists have broken through new and important inventions in the fight against cancer.	Invented or made something new.
Break through (2)	Luis Suarez broke through the defense of his rival team.	Found way/ forced a passage
Break up (1)	Our school will break up from next Saturday. The meeting broke up at 5 p.m.	close
Break up (2)	They **broke up** their relation and entered another soon.	(Ended relationship)
Break up into (3)	The ship was broken up into parts in the clash against the rock under water.	Separated or ruin
Break with	Everyone should break with the superstition about religion. There should be only one of Humanity. It means coexist, cooperation, tolerance, peace and prosperity for all living beings.	Give up
	Bring	
Bring about	Following blind ego, falsity, pretention and blind love for fantasy will bring about only our own ruin before time.	cause
Bring back (1)	I shall bring back the book tomorrow.	Return
Bring back (2)	The sight of the village brought back old memories.	Restored
Bring back to	The change of place brought him back to his health.	Restored to
Bring down	The price of essential commodities has been brought down a bit since last week.	reduced

Bring down	The enemy aircraft was brought down.	Force sth. down by firing
Bring forth/in	All trees bring forth new tender leaves during rainy season.	Produce /beget
Bring forward	All these matters were brought forward in the meeting for discussion.	Raised or presented
Bring in	My business brings in good income.	Yields/profits
Brings in (2)	They tried to bring new fashion in the publication.	introduce
Bring off	Our football team brought off a grand victory.	won
Bring on (1)	The damp weather has brought on his illness.	Led to.
Bring on (2)	He has brought on this disgrace to himself.	caused
Bring out	My first book brought out in 2013. It was a book of poems.	published
Bring out (2)	Proper training will bring out the best in him.	Reveal, nurture
Bring round (1)	The patient was brought round by careful nursing.	Made restored to
Bring round (2)	After proper counseling he was brought round.	Made cure to /overcome
Bring to	The girl fainted but was soon brought to.	bring her to conscious
Bring under	Her indomitable spirit can't be brought under.	subdued
Bring up	After the death of his father, he was brought up by his mother.	reared
	Burst	
Burst in	My friend burst in my house and informed of my father's accident.	Enter a room or building suddenly
Burst in sb	We were talking, then a beggar burst in us seeking help.	interrupted
Burst on	We were tensed of, when he burst on the scene.	Appeared suddenly
Burst forth	A tiger burst forth from the jungle	Came out

		suddenly
Burst into	The woman burst into tears at the news of her husband's death.	Fell in cry terribly
Burst open	The door burst open with a gust of wind and we could see only lightings around.	Open suddenly and violently
Burst out	He burst out weeping like a child.	

C *for* 'Call' 'Carry', 'Cast', 'Catch', 'Cheered', 'Clear', 'Come', 'Cry', 'Cut'

Group Verbs	Examples	Meanings
Call at... (of a train)	The train calls at Didcot & Reading.	To stop at a place for a short time
Call at (2)	We called him at his house.	met
Call away	She was called away from the meeting to receive an urgent phone call.	To ask sb to stop what they are doing and to go somewhere else
Call back	• She said she'd call back. • I'm waiting for Uday to call me back. • Call her back; she said it was urgent. • Do you call me back?	To telephone sb again; to telephone sb who telephoned you earlier
Call for (sth)	His mater called for an explanation of his conduct.	needed/ required sth
Call for (sb)	I'll call for you at 7 O'clock.	To collect sb to go somewhere
Call forth	Your speech called forth an angry response from him.	Elicited /produce a particular reaction
Call in (1)	He called in a doctor.	Sent for/ called for help or service
Call in (2)	The National Library has called in all overdue books.	Ordered the return of
Call off	The boss called off the meeting with us to attend the another.	(cancelled)
Call	I now call upon the chairman to	Invite or ask sb to

on/upon	address the meeting. I feel call upon to warn you about gambling.	speak/ feel that I ought
Call out	The fire brigade was called out by the authorities before it was too late.	Summoned /to ask sb to come in emergency
Call over	The students are called over by their roll numbers.	To give attendance
Call to	I called to my friend from the roof.	Addressed loudly
Call up (1)	Call up Rahim to save you from this crisis.	To make a telephone call to sb
Call up	She could not call up the verse and got zero marks.	Remember /to bring sth back to your mind
Call upon (2)	He was called upon to explain his conduct.	ordered
	Carry	
Carry about	He carries about a folding chair wherever he goes.	To take sth with
Carry away /off	He was carried away by his enthusiasm. The little dog was carried away by the current.	driven
Carry away (2)	Don't get carried away. Wait, there are more waiting...	Extremely excited
Carry back	The incident carried him back to his childhood days.	Returned to the past
Carry off (2)	Covid 19 has carried off many of our brother and sisters.	taken the lives of
Carry off	He carried off all the prizes. Nick carried off the best prize.	won
Carry on	I am carrying on the work while he is away.	continuing
Carry out (1)	I shall carry out what I have promised. However, I know I always forget.	fulfill
Carry out (2)	He agreed to carry out_my orders.	(execute)

Carry through	Only courage carried him through this crisis.	Helped him to overcome ...
Carry through	He carried through the work successfully.	completed
	Cast	
Cast about for	He is casting about for an opportunity to escape.	Looking for
Cast aside	He has cast aside his family for a foolish reason!	forsaken
Cast away (1)	He cast away his old clothes and entered the washroom.	Thrown away.
Cast away (2)	The ship was cast away_on the coast of Africa.	(wrecked)
Cast down	He is easily cast down. However, you can't say, he has tendency to commit suicide.	depressed
Cast off (sth)	I am trying to cast off my poor image, so that they think it twice.	Shun/ abandon
Cast out	If you come to me, I shall not cast you out.	reject
	Catch	
Catch at	A drowning man catches at a straw.	Try to seize
Catch on	She is very quick on to catch on to things. She is intelligent.	To grasp or understand sth
Catch out	Many investors were caught out by the fall in share price.	To surprise and put them in difficult situation
Catch up on	I have a lot of things to catch up on.	To spend extra time doing new things.
Catch up in	Innocent passers-by got caught up in the riots.	To become involved accidently
Catch up with	• Go on ahead; I'll catch up with you. • Don't wait for me. You guys go on. I will go on my bike & catch up with you soon.	To reach sb who is ahead by going faster than him.
Catch up with	Will India catch up with the developed countries?	To be in same level improving faster than others

	Cheer	
Cheer on	The audiences cheered the players on in the stadium.	To give shouts in encouragement in sports
Cheer up	• Oh, come on—cheer up! • Give Mary a call; she needs cheering up. • Bright curtains can cheer up a dull room.	To make sb or sth cheerful
	Clear	
Clear away/out	Ask the servant to ***clear away*** the table. The sweeper ***cleared out*** the drain.	To clean
Clear away (2)	The mist has cleared away after the sunrise.	dispersed
Clear off	Jack worked overtime to clear off arrears of work.	To finish or complete
Clear off (2)	Clear off from here.	Get out
Clear out (2)	Please, clear out my room.	Leave
Clear up	The sky is clearing up.	Gets rid of clouds/ becomes clear
	Come	
Come about	When did the accident come about? Can you tell me how it came about?	Happen/ take place
Come across (1)	He spoke for a long time; but his meaning didn't really come across.	To be understood /come over
Come across (1)	Kinsley came across his ex-girlfriend. He stepped forward and kissed her forehead to make surprise all there.	Met by chance
Come	Father came across the thing what	Found a thing by

across (2)	he had lost before five months.	chance
Come across (3)	I hoped she'd come across with some more information.	To provide or supply sth what you need
Come after	The night guard came after the thief; however, the thief escaped.	chased
Come along (1)	Come along, it is getting late.	hurry
Come along (2)	When the right opportunity comes along, she'll take it.	To arrive /appear
Come apart	The book just came apart in my hands.	To break into pieces
Come around	Your mother has not yet come round from the anesthetic.	Come to/to become conscious again
Come around (2)	Do come around and see us some time.	To visit a place a place for short time
Come around (3)	He'll never come around to our way of thinking.	Change one's mood or opinion
Come at (1)	She came at me with a knife. The rioters came at us last night with swords and others.	attacked
Come at (2)	We're getting nowhere—let's come at it from another angle.	To think about a problem or situation from different angle
Come away from	The plaster has started come away from the wall.	To become separated from
Come away with	We came away with the impression that all was not well with their marriage.	To leave a place with a particular feeling or impression
Come back	You came back very late last night.	Returned
Come back	Long hair for men seems to be coming back in.	To become popular again
Come before	The case comes before the court next week.	To be presented

Come between	I hate anything come between us.	Sth to damage a relationship
Come by (1)	She came by the house.	Made a short visit
Come by (2)	How did you come by his purse? Jobs are hard to come by these days.	(get)/obtain
Come down (1)	The new bridge came down after its inauguration in Kolkata. Minister says, "We look into the matters."	collapsed
Come down (2)	The rain came down in torrents.	fell
Come down from	She came down from Oxford.	To leave a university
Come down from	He has come down from North Bengal. He has come down from China.	From one place to another, generally from north to south.
Come down on	Don't come down so hard on her.	Criticize sb severely/ punish
Come down to	The name has come down from last century.	Sth that comes from long past
Come down with	I think I'm coming down with flu.	To get an illness that is not very serious.
Come forward	He came forward and offered his help.	(Voluntarily give help or information)
Come from	Where do you come from?	The place where sb lives
Come of	B. R. Ambedkar came of a poor family.	Was born in
Come off (1)	When will the festival come off?	Take place
Come off (2)	When I tried to lift the jug, the handle came off.	Became separated from
Come on (1)	The project is coming on nicely.	Growing

Come on (2)	Come on, we will be late for the function.	Hurry on
Come on (3)	The rainy season is coming on in the coastal areas.	Beginning
Come out (1)	The rain stopped and the sun came out.	appeared
Come out (2)	When is your next book coming out?	Publishing
Come over (1)	He will never come over to our side.	Change side
Come over (2)	Why did you come over here?	travelled
Come round	Father came round his sufferings soon, and began mix with us.	(recovered/cured)
Come through (1)	A message has come through here that are going to resign?	reached
Come through (2)	May your father come through soon.	Recover/ come round
Come upon	We came upon some boys playing in the field. We sought help from them.	Found by chance
	Cry	
Cry down	Don't cry down his achievements. Think, what labor he gave we can't.	Underestimate /decry
Cry off	We said we would go but we had to cry off at the last moment.	abandon
Cry to	The helpless man cried to the rioters for his life.	begged
Cry up	A trader cries up his own goods.	Extols/ exaggerates
Cry out	Peter cried out for help, none heard, none came.	Shouted loudly
Cry out against	People of one community often cry out against what they should not. None love patience is our destination!!	Protest sth
	Cut	
Cut away	They trimmed the plants, cutting away the uneven branches.	clipping
Cut down (1)	Please cut down your story. It is almost a novel in length.	Shorten

Cut down (2)	The physician advised him to cut down his consumption of animal protein.	reduce
Cut in	She kept on cutting in our conversation.	Interrupting
Cut off (1)	The baby is cut off from its mother.	Separated
Cut off (2)	He was cut off at an early age.	Died
Cut out (1)	One of the aircraft's engines cut out.	Stopped functioning
Cut out (2)	Maizie was cut out for this job.	Suitable
Cut out (3)	Sonny cut Sophia out in the competition.	defeated
Cut up (1)	The mother was terribly cut up at the death of her own son.	Upset
Cut up (2)	He cut up the bread.	Cut into pieces

D *for* deal, do, draw

Group Verbs	Examples	Meanings
Deal in (1)	He deals in rice.	Trades in
Deal in (2)	The book deals in detail about Phrase, Clause & sentences.	discusses
Deal out	The profits will be dealt out among the investors.	distributed
Deal with (1)	They try to deal politely with the customers.	Behave with
Deal with (2)	He dealt with the difficult problem easily.	Solved.
	Do	
Do away with (1)	'Why to do away with death penalty?' he said.	abolish
Do away with (2)	The woman tried to do away with herself.	Kill (also 'do in'
Do for (1)	The mutual disbelief does for	ruins

	any relation.	
Do for (2)	This piece of stick will do for a scale.	Serve or used as
Doff (contraction of 'do off')	Doff your coat.	Take off
Don (contraction of 'Do on')	Don your coat.	Put on
Do in (1)	The young actress was so depressed that she felt like doing in herself.	killing
Do in (2)	He looked very done it.	exhausted
Do over (1)	He was done over by a gang of anti-socials.	Attacked and injured severely.
Do over (2)	We are doing over the drawing room.	Having decorated
Do up (1)	Who is to do up your room every day?	arrange
Do up (2)	We are having the kitchen done up.	Repaired.
Do with (1)	We can no longer do with his insolvency. (Inability to pay due)	tolerate
Do with (2)	What will you do with these match sticks?	What use make of
Do with (3)	A politician has to do with all sorts of men.	Deal with
Do with (4)	Please return the book when done with.	Finished
Do without	He can hardly do without his private secretary.	Manage without

	Draw	
Draw away	His attention was drawn away by the loud noise.	Diverted.
Draw back	The chairman drew back declaring the time-table of the innings.	Receded/retreated
Draw in	The Rajdhani express is drawing in.	Entering the station
Draw on	Evening was drawing on.	Approaching
Draw out (1)	The girl is very shy and needs to be drawn out to talk.	Encouraged

Draw out (2)	The professor drew out the interview with MR. Rahaman intentionally to test his patience for the job.	prolonged
Draw to	I drew to Priya from the first day.	Felt attracted by
Draw up	He drew out the contract.	Wrote out
	Drop	
Drop away	His friends dropped away with his name growing.	Became fewer/drop off
Drop by	Some friends dropped by to see me.	Made short visits
Drop by	On his long journey, he **dropped by** at every metropolitan.	(Stopped for a visit)
Drop in	On my way back, I shall drop in at her house.	Pay a casual visit
Drop off	My friends dropped off one by one after we got marriage everyone.	Reduce in number/ became fewer
Drop off (2)	I always dropped off during the long prayer on each Sunday.	Fell asleep
Drop out		

Fall

Group Verbs	Examples	Meanings
Fall apart (1)	The glass **fell apart**.	(Broke into pieces)
Fall apart (1)	Their marriage finally fell apart.	broke
Fall away (1)	The film-star's fans fell away with the decline of his popularity.	Deserted /left him
Fall away (2)	The black spots are yet to fall away from your face.	Disappear
Fall away (3)	He has much fallen away since I saw him last.	Become lean
Fall back	The enemy fell back with the advance of our troops.	Retreated
Fall back	The army fell back upon a new line of	Had

upon	defense.	recourse to
Fall behind	France fell behind Germany in coal production.	Failed to keep level with
Fall for	Mr. P falls for every pretty face he sees only to see hardly any heart in them.	Yields to charm of
Fall in (1)	The game teacher asked his students to fall in.	Get into a line.
Fall in (2)	The new building fell in within a year.	Collapsed
Fall in with (1)	Subba fell in with his best friend Kanak in the fest after a decade.	Met by chance
Fall in with (2)	Finally, he fell in with our decision.	Agree/give consent
Fall off (1)	Attendance in classes has fallen off after the exams in schools.	Decreased
Fall off (2)	False friends fall off in misfortune.	Drop off
Fall on/upon (1)	Miscreants fell on/upon them.	Attacked fiercely
Fall on/upon (2)	The full cost of the ceremony fell on the students.	Incurred
Fall out	The boys fell out with each other with the issue of goal.	Quarreled
Fall through	Our holiday plans suddenly fell through.	Failed
Fall to	He fell to eating with greater gusto.	began

G *for* Get, Give, Go

Group Verbs	Examples	Meanings
Get about /around (1)	The news of our President's death gets about sooner than we hoped.	spread
Get about /around (2)	• The scandal of his affair with a widow got about in a day. • News soon got around that he had resigned.	Spread (as a rumor)
Get about /around (3)	She gets about/around with the help of a stick.	
Get across	Your meaning didn't really get across.	To be communicated /understood

Get ahead	• She wants to get ahead in her career. • Who doesn't want to get ahead? • She wanted so and she got ahead.	To make progress (further than others)
Get along with (1)	It is the right time to **get along with** your enemies all, and set up peace with them.	(To be friendly with someone)
Get along (2)	It's time we are getting along.	Leaving the place
Get at sb (1)	She's always getting at me.	Criticizing sb
Get at sth (2)	• The fox could not get at the grapes. • The files are locked up and I can't get at them.	Reach
Get at sth (2)	• In this situation, truth is hard to get at. • The truth is sometimes difficult to get at.	Find out
Get away (1)	We're hoping to get away for a few days at Easter.	To have a holiday or vacation
Get away (2)	• The prisoner got away last night. • Thieves got away with computer equipment worth three lacs.	Escaped
Get away (3)	• The culprit can't get away. • He can't get away with only imprisonment of three months! • No body can't get away insulting me like that.	Go unpunished /receive relatively light punishment
Get back (1)	• When did you get back last night? • When will you get back from there?	Return
Get back (2)	• She's got back her old job. • She got back her lost iPhone	To obtain sth again after

	after six months from riverbed.	having lost it
Get back at sb	• Finally, the rabbit **got back at** the rat and drove it away. • I'll find a way of getting back at him!	(To get revenge on somebody)
Get back in	• Jadavas finally got back in power in Bihar. • Will communist ever return in West Bengal.	To win election after having lost the prev. ones
Get back to sb	• I'll find out and get back to you. • She said she would get back to me within few days.	To speak or write again later as a reply
Get behind with	• I'm getting behind with my work. • He got behind with his profession.	Failing to make enough progress
Get by	Most of salary men here got by on a small salary.	Managed to live.
Get down (1)	Did you get down his address?	Write down
Get sb down	Saying that you only got him down.	Felt him depressed
Get sth down	I got the medicine down!	Swallow sth usually with great difficulty
Get down to (2)	Let's get down to our work.	Begin
Get in /into	• What time is the flight expected to get into Bagdogra from Chennai? • The train got in late.	Arrive
Get into (1)	• Father got me into the school.	Admitted
Get into (2)	• Don't get into a running train.	Enter
Get into (3)	• He got into trouble with police when he was still a student. • I got into conversation with a Italian student.	To become involved in/ to reach a condition
Get off (1)	Get off me, that hurts!	Tell sb to stop touching
Get off/ get sb off	• We got off straight after breakfast.	To leave

	• She got her child off to his school every day. • We got off in mid of the meeting.	
Get off to	I had great difficulty getting off to sleep.	To fall asleep
Get off with sb	• Steve got off with Tracey at the party. • Do the youths go there to go off with somebody?	To have sexual or romantic relation with sb
Get off (2)	We were lucky to get off.	Escape
Get on	I am getting on in my studies.	Making a good progress.
Get out (1)	His secret got out to all.	Became known
Get out (2)	Few passengers were lucky to get off from the burning train.	escape
Get over	The old man could not get over the shock of his son's death.	Overcome
Get round (1)	He knows well how to get round his first customers to his views.	Influence
Get round (2)	Do you find any way of getting round the problem?	Solving
Get through (1)	Many failed the test and few got through.	Passed
Get through (2)	Please join us as soon as you get through your personal task.	Complete
Get up (1)	What time does he get up?	Wake up
Get up (2)	The old lady slowly got up, went through the gate and disappeared.	Stood up
	Give	
Give away (1)	The chief guest along with others gave away the prizes on school sports day.	Distributed
Give away (2)	The soldier didn't give away any secret to our enemy.	Reveal
Give back	Could you give back my book?	return
Give forth	The engine gave forth a lot of smoke.	emitted
Give in	The powerful soldiers, somehow, **gave in**, and the citizens were saved	(surrendered)

	from the inevitable deaths by their hand.	
Give off	The fire **gave off** dense smoke.	(emitted)/give out
Give out (1)	After few days, our stock of rice will give out.	Exhaust
Give out (2)	The bust furnace is giving out a lot of heat.	Emitting
Give out (3)	The chairman gave out the new interest on HBL and FDs.	declared
Give over (1)	Before exams, most of students give over to their studies what they don't through the year.	Devoted himself
Give over (2)	The accused were given over to the police. The working PM gave over the charge to the new PM of the state.	Handed over
Give up (1)	You should give up smoking.	Stop
Give up (2)	Don't give up hope in difficult times. Give up bad habit if you want to improve your life.	abandon
	Go	
Go about	I hate this going about for the promotion of my book.	Moving about
Go about	A strong rumor is going about that he will leave us shortly.	Is in circulation
Go abroad	I never went abroad in my life time, and yet I am a refugee! Mr. Das often goes abroad to attend his business meeting.	Away from home, especially visit to a foreign country
Go after	The soldiers went after the enemy	Chased
Go against	The police will go against the public interest.	Oppose
Go along	As you go along, soon it will be found interesting.	Continue accepting
Go ahead	All arrangements are going ahead to celebrate the occasion.	Making progress
Go aside	Don't go aside from the path of virtue.	Deviate
Go at (1)	The two brothers go at each other at the slightest provocation.	attack
Go at (2)	They are going at it to complete the	Making the

	road in due time.	best possible effort.
Go away	The beggar has gone away with all his belongings.	Left the place
Go back upon/from	I cannot go back upon or from my word.	Fail to keep
Go beyond	You should not go beyond your limits.	Cross limit/exceed
Go by (1)	You cannot always **go by** appearances.	judge from /according to
Go by (2)	They talked of days gone by.	Past
Go by (3)	I shall go by what my teachers says. It is a good rule to go by.	To be guided by/follow order
Go down	The sun has gone down.	Sunset
Go down (2)	The price of butter has gone down.	Reduced
Go down (3)	Netaji is gone down as a great patriot.	Regarded as
Go down (4)	He has gone down with fever.	Suffered from
Go for	He goes for a scholar here, since he was a gold medalist in his graduation.	Regarded as
Go for (2)	Shall I go for a doctor?	Fetch/bring
Go in for	We shall go in for next B. Sc's exam.	Sit for
Go in for (2)	Public will go in for abolition of this custom.	Favor/support
Go off (1)	The bomb went off and many people were injured.	Exploded
Go off (2)	The party went off well.	Passed
Go off (3)	The pistol went off suddenly.	Was discharged
Go on	The meeting went on for ten minutes, and we left the place.	Continued
Go out (1 & 2)	Go out in the sun. The lamp has gone out after twelve minutes.	Go outside/ extinguished
Go over	He went over to opposition party.	Changed side
Go over	Please go over the accounts.	Examine

(2)		
Go through	I shall go through the papers.	Examine fully
Go through (2)	My father went through great suffering those twenty minutes, and he died.	Experienced
Go through (3)	I heard the proposal went through without any opposition.	Was accepted
Go up	The price of essential commodities is going up.	increasing
Go upon	He does not go upon any fixed principles.	Follow
Go with	I'll go with you in this matter.	Agree with
Go without	He has been going without food for five days.	Passed time except
	Grow	
Grow apart	The happiest couple grew apart from last year.	Stopped having a close relationship
Grow away from sb	They have grown away from each other; now they live at different places.	Become less close or depended
Grow back	The plant grew back in the rainy season.	
Grow up	Grow up man, why cry over love and love, a meaningless game on thy earth!	(To stop acting like a child)

H *for* Hand, Hang, Hold

Group Verbs	Examples	Meanings
Hand down	The custom has been handed down to the present generation.	Passed on to next generation
Hand in	The minister has handed in his resignation to the Governor.	Tendered/given /offered
Hand on	Hand on the book to your friend.	Pass on
Hand over	The accused was handed over to the police by the villagers.	Delivered
	Hang	
Hang about/around	The little child hangs about/around his father.	Remain close to

Hang about/around	Why do you hang about the examination hall?	Move suspiciously close to sth/sb
Hang back	I am not here to hang back from my place.	Go back
Hang down	He hung down his head with shame; but I was shameless! I kept my head up.	Bowed down one's head
Hang on (1)	I do not like to hang on others for my bread.	Depend on
Hang on (2)	Through these years I hanged on in the project.	Stuck to someone/somet hing
Hang on (3)	Would you hang on a minute, please?	Wait
Hang on (4)	He hung on until we put him down.	Hanging from sth
Hang out (1)	People hung out flags to welcome the Prime Minister.	displayed
Hang out (2)	We **hanged out** in the boat whole night and passed a pleasant night with thousand stars over our heads.	(To spend a lot of time with someone in a place)
Hang over (1)	Do not hang over the open balcony.	To bend down
Hang over (2)	The meeting has been hung over.	postponed
Hang together	You should all hang together and achieve success.	Support one another
Hang up (1)	A notice was hung up on the wall.	Put up/suspend
Hang up (2)	I cut short the telephone conversation and hung up.	Replaced the receiver
Hang upon	The crowd hung upon the leader's words.	Listened attentively to
Hold		
Hold back (1)	**Hold back** your wrath! It is improper to **pass over** us like that!	(To stop yourself from doing

		something)
Hold back (2)	• **Hold back** your weakness from your dear ones, and you are safe. • Truth can never be held back.	(hide/conceal)
Hold by	• Only friends held by in your difficult time.	Adhered to
Hold in	Hold in your temper. None here to bear with.	Check
Hold off (1)	Milo should hold off from such agitation.	Keep aloof/ maintain distance from
Hold on (1)	Please hold on for a minute.	Wait
Hold on (2)	The rain held on for two hours.	Continued
Hold on (3)	We should hold on the course through all opposition.	Stick to
Hold out (1)	She always held out her helping hands to known and unknown.	Extended
Hold out (2)	The doctor held out little hope of his recovery.	Promised/assured/gave
Hold up	He **held up** long hours and we were about to lose our patience.	(delayed)
Hold with	They hold with us in this matter.	agree

K *for* Keep, Knock

Group Verbs	Examples	Meanings
Keep at	We need to keep at our principles.	Stick to
Keep away/off	Keep away from bad company. Fire keeps off wild animals.	Keep aloof
Keep back	I never kept back anything from my lover.	Concealed
Keep down	You must keep down your anger.	Control/ suppress
Keep from	Keep from bad habits.	Refrain
Keep in (1)	It is wise to keep in while it is lighting.	Stay indoors
Keep in (2)	The fire will keep in till tomorrow.	Continue burning
Keep in (3)	Are they able to keep in with us anymore after the incident?	Agree with us
Keep off	Alertness keeps off many dangers.	Wards off
Keep on	Keep on. You must reach your goal.	Continue

Keep out	I was kept out of the business.	Put me outside
Keep to	You should always keep to your principles.	Adhere to
Keep under	Please keep your temper under control.	Keep in check
Keep up	Skipper Cook always kept up pressure on the Indian team.	Maintained
Keep up with	You must keep up with the changing world.	Keep pace with
	Knock	
Knock about	Employees of Central Govt. have no fixed place to live in, they knock about at different places.	Leads an unsettled life
Knock down	He was knocked down by taxi.	Hit by
Knock down	The building was knocked down.	Broken down
Knock off	The workers usually knock off at five o'clock.	Stop work
Knock off	The shopkeeper will knock off thousand rupees if you want to buy the Peter's book.	Deduct
Knock out	Mary Kom knocked out her opponent in the next two rounds.	Defeated
Knock out	I was knocked out by the news.	Overwhelmed
Knock sb up	Please knock me up at five O'clock.	Make wake up
Knock up sth	Mother knocked up a meal for us.	Prepared hurriedly
Knock up	He was knocked up after work of five hours.	Tired/ exhausted

L *for* **lay, Let, look** & *miscellaneous*

Group Verbs	Examples	Meanings
Lap sth up	It's a terrible movie but audiences everywhere are lapping it up.	Accept or receive sth with great enjoyment
Lap sth up	The calf lapped up the bucket of	Drink all of sth

	milk.	with great enjoyment
Lapse into	• She lapsed into silence again. • The patient lapsed into Coma soon after the accident.	Gradually pass into a worse or less active state or condition
Lark about /around	They larked about the last few months and now making complaints of their poor result.	Enjoyed themselves behaving in silly ways
Lash out at	Maizie suddenly lashed out at the boy without any provocation.	To suddenly try to hit sth or sb
Lash out at	In an article Peter lashed out at his all critics.	To criticize in an angry way
Laugh at sb	The experts laugh at my accent; but my don't care attitude ignores them always. / Don't laugh at me.	Making jokes of sb/ridicule
Laugh off	• I laughed off his suggestion of my resign from the post. • When something is likely to be beyond your patience, learn to laugh off them.	Didn't take sth serious and laugh them away

	Lay	
Lay about	He began to lay about him in anger.	Deal blows
Lay aside	We need to lay aside something for our bad days.	Keep apart/ cast aside
Lay by/in	Lay by something for the future.	Store up for future use
Lay down	Our freedom fighters laid down their lives to the cause of the country's liberation.	Sacrificed
Lay down (2)	No such rules are laid down in the book of Constitution.	Written
Lay in/by/up	Hoarders laid in food for the future. He laid up enough for the future.	Stored
Lay off	Some workers were laid off for their agitation.	suspended
Lay on (1)	The mother laid her hand on her son's head.	Put
Lay on (2)	Taxes at highest rate were laid on liquid.	imposed
Lay out	He laid out his all in the business.	Expended

Lay out (2)	The garden is well laid out.	Arranged/ decorated
Lay up	I am laid up with fever.	Confined to bed
	Let	
Let sb down (1)	The machine won't let it down.	Fail to help or support
Let sb/sth down (2)	Edith speaks French very fluently, but her pronunciation lets her down, like Peter to his English.	Make sb/sth less successful than they or it should be
Let sb in	What let her in this situation?	Make sb involved in
Let in	Let him in.	(allow sb to enter)
Let sb off	Let her off all these. This is our business. Whatever let me face.	Allow sb not to do
Let sb off	She was let off with a warning. They were our cousins. They let us off lightly.	Not punish sb/ give them only light punishment
Let sb out	• Being her friends, it is our business to let her out of this situation. • Counselling is very important to let her out from this worse condition.	To make sb not to feel alone/ help someone to come out depression
Let out	Suddenly she let out a scream of terror. There was a long snake facing towards her eyes.	To give a cry out of excitement of joy or sorrow
Let up	The pain finally let up.	To become less strong
Let up (2)	We mustn't let up now.	To make less effort
	Look	
Look about for	Charlotte is looking about for a house in the new town.	Searching for/look for
Lok after	Parents look after their children out	Take care of

	of love.	
Look at	Look at the birds sitting on the tower.	Gaze at/ask to see
Look down upon/at	• He **<u>looks down at</u>** them as they were his eternal slaves, and he is the Lord, equal of God. • Don't look down upon the poor.	Humiliate /deride
Look for	We looked for better treatment from your son-in-law	Expected
Look for (2)	I am looking for the file which has yellow cover.	Searching for
Look forward to	We looked forward to our uncle' s visit during that time. He brought gifts and blessings for us all.	Expecting with pleasure
Look in	I shall look in his house when I pass by his.	Pay a short visit
Look into	Don't worry. I'll look into the matter soon.	Enquire into
Look on/ upon (1)	We looked upon you only as our well-wishers, but we were wrong.	regarded
Look on (2)	The house looked on to the river. The balcony looks on the river.	Faced/overlooks
Look out for	The police were looking out for the criminal. The eagle is looking out for a prey.	Watch/search for
Look over	The authority looked over his application and finally sanctioned his leave for two months.	examined
Look through	Please look through the letter and say, where are mistakes.	Examine carefully
Look to (1)	Look to your own affairs.	Attend
Look to (2)	I look to you for help.	Rely on
Look up (1)	Pamela **<u>looked up</u>** and asked nothing.	Saw up
Look up (2)	Prices of all things including essential commodities are looking up since few months, and there is no extra income or DA.	Increasing /rising
Look up (3)	Please look us up while returning from London.	Visit
Look up (4)	Look up a nearest meaning of the word in dictionary.	Find out

Look up (5)	After a dull period, Peter's business is looking up.	improving
Look up to	I look up to him as my elder brother.	respect

Make

Group Verbs	Examples	Meanings
Make after	The Royal Bengal tiger made after the deer was a terrible sight in our last trip in Sundarbans.	chased
Make away with	Farah made away with her own life.	destroyed
Make for	I made for Delhi, then I had to call off , and I got down at Kanpur Station to return.	Started a journey
Make of	What do you make of the word?	Understand
Make off	The new bride made off with all ornaments in the house.	Escaped
Make out	I could not make out what he said.	Understand
Make out	Make out a list of your books.	Prepare
Make over	The going principal made over charge me.	Delivered /hand over
Make up (1)	Who make up this loss?	Compensate
Make up (2)	More two boys will make up the team.	Complete
Make up (3)	We made up our quarrel.	Made understanding
Make up (4)	They made up (their minds) to return.	decided

P *for* Pass, Pick, Pull, Put & others

Group Verbs	Examples	Meanings
Pass away (1)	The clouds have passed away.	dispersed
Pass away	My old grandfather died last week.	Died

(2)		
Pass by (1)	We pass by her house every day.	Go by
Pass by (2)	We should not pass by our younger's faults.	Overlook /ignore
Pass for	He is passed for a great scholar.	Regarded
Pass off (1)	The train has passed off.	Ceased gradually
Pass off (2)	He should be punished for trying to pass off false coins.	Deceive with
Pass off well	The ceremony passed off well.	Was a success
Pass of worse	The ceremony passed off worse.	Was unsuccessful
Pass on	Let us pass on another subject.	Proceed
Pass over	My claim was passed over.	Neglected/ turn down
Pass through (1)	Crude oil passes through the pipe.	Goes through
Pass through (2)	The crew of the boat **passed through** terrible sufferings.	(underwent)/ experienced
	Pick	
Pick at/on	Why do you always pick at/on me?	Find fault with
Pick out (1)	• Can you pick out the adverbs in the following sentences? • Can you pick out the culprits in the gathering? • **Pick out** the correct word from the options, and fill in the blanks.	Identify /choose
Pick out (2)	He picked up Italian tune in the piano.	Played
Pick up (1)	Where did you pick up your English?	Learn
Pick up (2)	The smugglers were picked up by the police.	Arrested
Pick up (2)	Do you pick the bags from my aunt while returning?	Collect
Pick up (3)	I asked her to pick me up on her way to home.	To give a lift
Pick up (4)	Share price has forgotten to pick up long days.	Improve in business
Pick up (5)	Where did you pick up malaria?	Effected by

Pick up (6)	Suddenly the car picked up speed and disappeared.	Gathered
Pick up (7)	Our TV cannot pick up all these channels. We don't have cables.	Receive
Pick up (8)	I fell ill during COVID-19, but soon picked up.	Recovered
	Others	
Point out	He **pointed out** the audiences with his views and secured his victory in the coming election.	drew attention to
	Pull	
Pull at	The workers are pulling at the heavy machine.	Trying to remove
Pull apart	Failing to yield me, they started pulling me apart.	Criticize unfavorably
Pull down (1)	The municipal authority decided to pull down the old buildings in the locality to avoid further loss of lives.	Demolish
Pull down (2)	He looks much pulled down.	Lowered in health or spirits
Pull in (1)	He is pulling in a lot of money publishing books new every day.	Earning
Pull in (2)	He was pulled in by SEBI for questioning.	Detained/arrested
Pull in (3)	The train pulled in on time.	Entered the platform
Pull off (1)	Pull off the cover and see what's in.	Remove
Pull off (2)	Our team pulled off a brilliant victory.	achieved
Pull out of (1)	The train pulled out of the station.	Left
Pull out of (2)	He was pulled out of difficult situations.	Come out from
Pulled out from	The lorry pulled out from behind the car.	Over crossed

Pull over	The driver **pulled over** the bus in the last second and saved us all.	(Moved the vehicle to one side of a road and stopped)
Pull through (1)	He is in great difficulties; but he will pull through if we offer him a little help.	overcome
Pull through (2)	He was critically ill, but has pulled through.	Recovered
Pull together	It will be done in a week, if we do it pulling together.	Working in harmony
Pull up (1)	I pulled up, as I saw a traffic police showed his hands.	Stopped
Pull up (2)	He was pulled up for his misbehavior.	Reprimanded /scolded
Pull up with	Initially he was trailing but soon he pulled up with others.	Improved relatively

Put		
Put about	I hear many stories that are being put about.	Spreading rumors
Put across	Jacob failed to put across his views to the commission.	Communicate successfully
Put aside (1)	We all need to put aside some amount of money for future use.	Save
Put aside (2)	Put aside your work and listen to me.	Stop sth for a time
Put away (1)	Put away enough money for your son's education.	Lay aside/ put aside/ save
Put away (2)	I tried much but had to put away the idea of buying a car of my own.	Give up/ abandon
Put away (3)	The patient was suffering much and finally he had to be put away with a legal permission.	Put death
Put back	Put back the book in its proper place.	Restore
Put by	Ants put by some food for the winter. Why shouldn't we?	Preserve/accu mulate
Put down (1)	The rebellion can't be put down by the govt.	Suppressed
Put down (2)	Put down only the names of the first and second according to group event.	Write
Put forth (1)	I put forth all my energy in this task, and could modify it in seven days.	Exerted

Put forth (2)	Trees put forth new leaves in the rainy season.	Generates
Put forward	One member of the house put forward the proposal to be considered.	Introduced
Put forward (2)	Dr. R.D. put forward a new theory on solar energy it may bring a revolution.	Advanced
Put in (1)	I have put in my claim before the commission.	Submitted
Put in (2)	Mr. Dutta has put in twenty years' service in teaching.	completed
Put in (3)	I could not put in a word among them.	Utter a word/ say sth.
Put in (4)	Please, put in a good word for me.	Plead on my behalf
Put off (1)	The meeting was put off.	Postponed
Put off (2)	Getting back home we put off our clothes.	Removed
Put on (1)	Put on your dress, we'll go out a long drive.	wear
Put on (2)	You needn't put on a gentle man.	disguise
Put on (3)	The blame was put on me.	Charged upon
Put on (4)	He has put on a lot of weight. Peter and Om put on ninety runs.	added
Put out (1)	The fire brigade team successfully put out the fire.	Extinguished
Put out (2)	The death of the General put out the soldiers.	Dishearten
Put out (3)	He is a good man. He always puts out his hand for others.	Offers help
Put out (4)	He put out his hand to take the book from table.	Stretched out
Put out (5)	Eyes of Pithwiraj Chowhan were put out in the camp of enemies.	Taken out /drawn out
Put through (1)	The task was put through twelve months.	Carried out
Put through (2)	After many attempts, the Internet connection was put through.	Established /run through

Put through (3)	The trainers in Military Academy had to put through rigorous schedule.	Had to undergo
Put up (1)	Rahul Dravid was a depending player who could put up a stiff resistance against rough bowlers in Test matches.	offer
Put up (2)	A notice is to put up soon regarding this.	Hung up
Put up (3)	Put up a fence round the garden.	raise
Put up (4)	I am putting up with my friend.	Staying for sometime
Put up with	None can put up with such kind of behavior.	tolerate

Run

Group Verbs	Examples	Meanings
Run about	The children started to run about in great panic.	Hurry from one place to another
Run across	I ran across my old friend in the ceremony after a decade about.	Met by chance
Run after	The police ran after the thief; they caught and carried him by neck and shoulder.	Pursued
Run after (2)	Do not run after money; but who listens to the words?	Pursuit/hunt for
Run against	Peter is running against odd situations with the shop keepers.	Fighting against
Run along	Now, children, run along!	Be off/run
Run at	The tiger runs at the deer.	Chased
Run away	Leo ran away and joined the army.	Left home
Run away with	The dog ran away with a piece of meat.	Fled with /stole
Run away with	The business proposal will run away with a lot of money.	Lead to expense
Run-away	They had a run-away victory in the match. (run-away victory= an idiom)	Easy/an easy task
Run down (1)	The tiger ran down the fox and punished it with death.	Catch by chase
Run down (2)	• Mother looks much run down through works for three hours.	Exhausted /run out

	• The battery has exhausted.	
Run down (3)	The man was run down by a reckless lorry on the rajpath.	Run over down
Run into (1)	He ran into debt.	Fell in debt.
Run into (2)	The bus ran into the railing.	Collide with
Run into (3)	The publication has run into ten editions.	Continued
Run into (4)	I met an old friend in the journey.	Met unexpectedly
Run off	The thief saw a policeman and ran off.	fled
Run on (1)	Our discussion ran on for hours together.	continued
Run on (2)	The engine runs on CNG.	Work on
Run out	• The stock of food ran out. • Water ran out of the tank. • The garrison didn't surrender until provisions ran out.	Exhausted
Run over (1)	An old man was run over by a lorry.	Knocked down
Run over (2)	In rainy season, the water of the river runs over its banks every year.	overflows
Run over (3)	She ran over the pages before entering the examination hall.	Glanced over hastily
Run through	Bullets ran through the body of the escaping terrorist.	Pierced
Run through (2)	I ran through the book and bought one for me.	Examine quickly
Run through (3)	Most of us, we run through our fortune for a chance of a Govt. appointment.	Use up /waste
Run to	The money required for the promotion run to a few lacs of rupees.	amount
Run up (1)	The boys ran up a flag on the pole.	Hoisted
Run up (2)	Our long stay at the Daman Diu Hotel ran up a big bill.	Caused to grow quickly
Run up (3)	Price of petrol ran up to Rs- 112. This is the third time within a month.	increased
Run upon	The cyclist ran upon the lamp post	Collided

(1)	and broke his thin helmet.	with
Run upon (2)	I ran upon a new idea to publish many booklets upon English Grammar to make them handy.	Be engrossed with

S *for* See, Send, Set, Stand & Others

Group Verbs	Examples	Meanings
See about	I must see about lunch. I will see about your proposal.	Prepare/consider
See about	He says he won't help, does he? Well, we'll soon see about that.	To deal with sth/ Will secure that he will...
See in	• I don't know what she finds in him. • What did you see in that black spot?	Find sb/sth attractive or interesting
See off	I'll go to the station to see off my friend.	To bid farewell going up to station airport etc. who is starting a journey.
See off (2)	The home team saw off the challengers by 68 runs.	Defeat sb in a gme or fight
See out	I've had this coat for y, and I'm sure it will see me out. The car has enough fuel to see our destination out.	Run till end of life or term/ to last longer than
See over	We need to see over the house again before we can give you the offer.	To visit a place to judge it carefully, valuation, worth, etc
See through	Her courage and humor saw her through	Let her considered or allowed/ to give help or support
See to	Will you see to the arrangements for our next meeting?	To deal with sth.
	Send	
Send away/off	I'm sending the files off to my boss tomorrow.	To send sth to a place by post or mail
Send down/up	We should send him down for his misbehavior.	Send sb to prison
Send for	Please send for a doctor.	Call for/summon

Send forth sth	He opened his mouth and send for a stream of noise.	To produce a sound or signal, so that other can hear
Send off	The data I sent off to my H.M. has not reached to him.	To send sth by post or mail
Send on	We sent our furniture on a ship. They sent theirs on an airship, but it couldn't reach ever for it struck accident in the mid of air.	To send sth to a place so that it arrives before you get there.
Send out	Have the invitations been sent out yet?	To send sth to a lot of people or place
Send up	Fifty boys have been sent up for higher studies in Canada.	Send sb to a place for higher study or to prison
	Set	
Set about	Paul set about packing since morning.	Began
Set aside (1)	The High Court set aside the judgement of the lower court.	Cancelled
Set aside (2)	Mother sets aside some money to spend in need.	Save for a time being
Set by	The beggar set by a huge amount of money by begging.	Saved
Set down (1)	The car set me down on the way.	Left me descend
Set down (2)	The police set down the complaint of the woman.	Recorded
Set forth (1)	Leon sets forth his views in his books.	exhibits
Set forth/off /out	• Sophia set forth her journey in last November. • Nicole set off for Japan. • Dean set out for England last week.	Started/leave for
Set off (2)	The frame set off the picture.	Increase beauty
Set off (3)	The gains were set off against losses.	balanced

Set in	The rainy season has set in.	Started/begun
Set on/upon	The dogs were immorally set upon the convict.	Let attack
Set out (1)	They set out for the picnic spot early in the morning.	Started/ leave for
Set out (2)	He set out his goods for display.	disperse
Set to/in	Let us set to work at once.	begin
Set up (1)	They set up a new school.	founded
Set up (2)	The local people set Ramesh up as their candidate in the Panchayat election.	Present/produce
Set up (3)	They set up hue and cry.	Raised
Set up (4)	He set up as a lawyer.	Began a profession
	Stand	
Stand against	All the members of the staff committee stood against the decision of the principal.	Opposed
Stand aside	Please stand aside to let the chairman pass.	Give place
Stand aside	He stood aside from the contest.	Took off/withdrew his name
Stand at	The total contribution so far stands at Rs ten thousand.	Is equal to
Stand by (1)	He will always stand by me.	Support
Stand by (2)	I merely stood by when they fought.	Was a silent onlooker/ stand off
Stand by (3)	In this tumultuous situation, the army is standing by to support the civil authorities.	Being ready
Stand for	White stands for purity. The letter 'L' stands for 'Learning.'	Symbolizes
Stand in (1)	The hero is absent; you are asked to stand in for him.	To be substitute
Stand in (2)	This is a pretty big amount; let me stand in with you.	Share expenditure
Stand off	I stood off from the debate.	Didn't participate in

from		
Stand out	Her performance stood out from the rest.	Was prominent/ conspicuous
Stand over	The question will stand over for the present.	Left for later settlement
Stand to	We should stand to our principles.	Stick to
Stand up for	They are determined to **stand up for** their rights.	(vindicate)/support
Stare at	The little boy is **staring at** us.	(Looking fixedly)

T *for* Take, Tell, Turn

Group Verbs	Examples	Meanings
Take aback	I was taken aback at the news of his insult in public.	surprised
Take after	The child takes after its mother.	Looks after/resembles
Take away	Do not take away books from the shelf.	remove
Take back	I will not take back my words.	Withdraw/take off
Take by	The dog took the cat by its neck.	Caught by
Take down (1)	Take down the names of the students	Register/write down/record
Take down (2)	Take down the book from the shelf.	Take a thing from up
Take (sb) for	Everyone took him for an honest man.	Consider/regard as
Take from	This will take from your reputation as a teacher.	lower
Take in (1)	He has taken in this plot of land for a garden.	enclosed
Take in (2)	I was taken in by the grocer.	cheated
Take in (3)	I cannot take in the meaning of the passage.	understand

Take in (4)	We shall take in 100 boys this year.	admit
Take into	Before selecting him, his health has to be taken into consideration.	To be considered
Take off (1)	The boy took off his shoes after return from his school.	Put off
Take off (2)	Do not take off a lame man.	mimic
Take off (3)	The plane will take off at 7 a.m.	Start flying
Take off (4)	Take your hands off my shoulders.	Remove/move off
Take off (5)	The morning bus service will be taken off the route from next week.	withdrawn
Take on	I decided to take on extra job for a better livelihood.	Undertake
Take (sb) on	I shall take you on at table tennis, though at other time we are two best friends.	Accept as an opponent
Take out	Take out the aching tooth.	remove
Take over	The new President will take over the charge of the government on next month of November.	Accept
Take to (1)	The young boy has taken to drinking recently.	(been) addicted to
Take to (2)	I took to the boy from the first.	Became fond of
Take up (1)	He took up my case.	Adopted/accepted
Take up (2)	Mr. Peter took up the problem to solve it.	Undertook
Take up (3)	The car takes up too much place. We will replace it with a mini one.	occupies
Take up (4)	He takes up a pen and began to write.	Takes
Take up (5)	I shall take the matter up with the principal and let's see what can be done.	Present /produce
Take up with	I was taken up with a book.	Absorbed in
Take upon	He took upon himself the burden of the family.	Took responsibility

Tell

Tell against	The evidence told against the accused.	Did harm to
Tell off (1)	The superintendent told off six policemen to guard his own quarter after the threat of death.	Selected and appointed to a special duty.
Tell off (2)	The teacher told him off for quarreling with his class-mates.	Spoke angrily/rebuke
Tell on/upon	Smoking started to take upon his health.	Affect
	Turn	
Turn about	The boys turned about and hurried for home.	Cancelled the programme
Turn against	I do not know why he turned against me.	Became hostile to
Turn away (1)	The sight pained me and I turned away.	Turned my face
Turn away (2)	Turn away the idea from your mind.	dismiss
Turn aside	We should not turn aside from the path of honesty.	Deviate
Turn back	Don't turn back a beggar from your door.	Send back/reject to give anything
Turn down	The principal has turned down our proposal.	Reject
Turn in (1)	I turned in early last night.	Went to bed
Turn in (2)	We saw a hut and turned in for shelter.	Entered in passing
Turn off	Turn off the switch.	Shut
Turn on (1)	Turn on the switch.	open
Turn on (2)	The case turns on his report.	Depends on
Turn out (1)	The man must be turned out from here. He is continuously making nuisance.	Driven out
Turn out (2)	His story turned out to be the best in the competition.	Proved
Turn out (3)	The people turned out in large numbers to see the sight.	assembled
Turn out	The mill turns out 100 pair of	produces

(4)	clothes every day.	
Turn to	Turn to God and He will save you.	Pray/surrender
Turn up	A huge crowd turned up for the match.	appeared

Use, Work, Write

Group Verbs	Examples	Meanings
Use up	**Use up** your nails and pail to reach your goal.	(To use completely)
Work at	The carpenter is working at the chair.	Engaged in making
Work in (1)	The water has worked in all round the packing box.	Penetrated
Work in (2)	Please try to work in a few more illustrations on the subject.	Introduce
Work off (1)	You must work off the accumulated work.	Dispose of/reduce
Work off (2)	Unless you work off your excess fat, you will fall ill.	Get rid of
Work on (1)	The engine works on diesel.	Runs by burning
Work on	The workers worked on day and night and the road was made complete in record time indeed.	Continued working on
Work out (1)	Yes, finally it **works out**. He agreed with us.	exercises/proves successful
Work out (2)	I still cannot work out the sum.	solve
Work out (3)	I have worked out your share of Rs 10 lac.	Calculate
Work out (4)	The scientists have worked a medicine to cure cancer completely.	Discover/find out
Work out (5)	The players are working out in the field before the match begins.	Undergoing exercise
Work up	The mob were worked up by his fiery speech.	excited
	Write	
Write down	Write down your name and address on a piece of paper.	Record
Write (sb) down	You can write him down as a useless fellow.	Take him to be

Write off (1)	Write off a short account of your performance in last one year in the previous company.	Prepare quickly
Write off (2)	The loss was written off.	Cancelled in writing/taken as recovery not possible.
Write out	Please, write out your name and address.	Write in full
Write up	He needs to write up some lines for my published books.	Write with praise

4. The Idioms

29. We have already studied, there are different kinds of phrases- from Noun to adjective and verb to Adverb. Some of these phrases, as Nominal, Relative, Adverbial, Prepositional and many of Phrasal verbs have their special uses in the English language since long past, they are called **'Idioms'**.

- So, idioms are not only from phrasal verbs but may be prepositional, nominal, relative or adverbial (as ***'by hook or by crook'***, ***'off & on'***, etc.). They sometimes may form an object to the verb, a complement, or other. Carefully study the examples and their roles in the sentences. For this, you may analyze a sentence too, for your better understanding.

- **Study the Idioms & their meanings, begins with 'A':**

1. On the question of dowry-system we are ***at one*** *(of the same opinion—[complement])*.
2. It is ***all one*** *(just the same)* to me whether I stay at Balurghat or go to Delhi.
3. The matter is now ***above board*** *(open or openly-[relative phrase])*, and anybody can see and comment on it.
4. The storm broke out ***all of (on) a sudden*** *(suddenly-[adv. phrase])*.

5. I was quite ***at sea*** *(perplexed)* in this matter.
6. It was ***all but*** *(very nearly, almost)* impossible.
7. The man thinks himself to be, ***as it were*** *(like, as if)*, the lord of the earth.
8. He is ***at his wit's end*** *(completely puzzled)* in the face of trouble.
9. He is ***all in all*** *(the supreme man)* in hi locality.
10. The sale of the book is ***at a low ebb*** *(diminishing)*.
11. He is not ***at all*** *(in any degree)* a scholar.
12. She comes to my house ***at times*** *(occasionally)*.

13. Do not waste time, as your examination is ***at hand*** *(close by, about to happen)*.
14. "I immediately felt ***at home*** *(feeling at ease)*."
15. The rebels surrendered ***at discretion*** *(unconditionally)*.
16. Keep bad companions ***at arm's length*** *(at a distance)*.
17. They are ***at dagger's drawn*** *(highly enraged at, in open enmity with)* with each other.
18. The cat is ***at bay*** *(in a dangerous position, in a tight corner)* in the room and so turns back to attack.
19. He can teach Grammar 36 hours ***at a stretch*** *(continue without break)*.
20. I am ***at a loss*** *(puzzled)* and find no way to escape from this situation.
21. His eldest son is ***a thorn in his side*** *(a constant source of annoyance)*.
22. All the problems of Mathematics are ***at his fingers' ends*** *(ready knowledge)*.
23. This savings will do ***at a pinch*** *(in case of emergency)*.
24. The articles in the room were ***at sixes and sevens*** *(in disheveled condition)*.

25. We reached the station ***at the eleventh hour*** *(at the last hour)*.
26. The beggar on road side is ***as good as*** *(similar to, practically no more than)* dead.
27. The life of the discoverer of an unknown land was ***at stake*** *(in a dangerous position)*.
28. He seems to be a worthless person ***at the first blush*** *(at first sight)*.
29. I am afraid you two friends are ***at cross-purposes*** *(misunderstand each other)*.
30. He works ***against time*** *(with utmost speed)*.
31. He wanted that everybody would be ***at his beck and call*** *(under one's absolute control)*.

32. I can sing many Bollywood songs ***after a fashion*** *(to a certain degree, not much).*
33. The woman is ***an ugly customer*** *(a difficult person to deal with).*
34. This book would not be ***a drug in the market*** *(unsalable for lack of demand).*
35. Throughout the lectures of Peter, the students are ***all ears*** *(deeply attentive)* in the seminar hall.
36. I was ***all eyes*** *(eagerly watching)* to see our C.M. but her speech only disheartened.

37. This land is ***a bone of contention*** *(a subject of dispute)* between two brothers in the family.
38. This act is ***a dead letter*** *(no longer in force)*, let us know new one.
39. It is ***a far cry*** *(long way of)* from Balurghat to London.
40. It is ***a far cry*** *(no easy transition)* from Capitalism to Communism.
41. The bank would not accept ***a man of straw*** *(a man of no substance, poor)* as a guarantor.
42. Unemployment is ***a hard nut to crack*** *(a difficult problem to solve)* eternal.
43. watching short-clips videos were ***all the rage*** *(very popular)* in certain times.
44. The police are on ***a wild goose chase*** *(a fruitless search)* to catch the thief.
45. You can rely on him; a he is ***a man of his words*** *(a trustworthy person).*
46. Only a few years ago he entered the firm and he is now ***at the top of the tree*** *(at the head of profession).*
47. This is the point ***at issue*** *(in dispute).*
48. The death of his wife was ***a bolt from the blue*** *(a sudden unexpected event)* to him.

❑ **Study the Idioms & their meanings, begins with 'B':**

49. I know he will do the job ***by hook or by crook*** *(by any means).*
50. There is ***bad blood*** *(ill feeling)* between the two families.
51. The secret of the case has been ***brought to light*** *(disclosed)* by the police.

52. ***Birds of a feather*** *(of the same nature or kind)* flock together.
53. One should know that the life is not a ***bed of roses*** *(a very comfortable situation)*.
54. He ***bids fair*** *(seems likely)* to rival his brother as a doctor.
55. He only ***beats about the bush*** *(talk irrelevantly)* in telling the story.
56. I saw him to be ***beside himself*** *(out of one's minds)* with grief.
57. He visits the place ***by fits and starts*** *(irregularly)*.
58. The price of essential commodities is increasing ***by leaps and bounds*** *(very swiftly)*.
59. Mr. P was ***behind the scenes*** *(in the off side of the event)* of the successful drama.
60. ***By the bye (way)*** *(incidentally)* he asked me about the nature of my job.
61. Seeing the accident his ***blood ran cold*** *(to be horrified)*.

62. The people of the village are ***by and large*** *(generally speaking, on the whole)* peasants.
63. He is ***by far*** *(in every respect)* an honest man.
64. He is ***by long odds*** *(most decidedly)* the best poet of the country.
65. Mr. G is one of the ***big guns*** *(a leading personality)* of the locality.
66. The miscreants ***beat*** the traveler ***black and blue*** *(beat severely)*.
67. The chief minister took a ***bird's eye view*** *(a superficial conception)* of the flood-stricken area from a helicopter.
68. She is a ***book worm*** *(who only reads book)*, and does nothing except reading.
69. He was ***brought to book*** *(gave punishment)* by the Head master for his offence.
70. The General of the enemy soldiers agreed to ***bury the hatchet*** *(cease fighting)*.
71. A modest man never ***blows his own trumpet*** *(praising oneself)*.
72. He wants to leave the place ***bag and baggage*** *(with all belongings)*.
73. She wastes her time by ***building castles in the air*** *(indulge in doing fictitious things)*.

74. His observations on the subject were ***beside the mark*** *(irrelevant)*.
75. Corruption as well as unemployment is a ***burning question*** *(matter of great importance)* today.
76. There are ***black sheep*** *(men of bad character)* in every community.

77. He ***burnt his fingers*** *(get oneself into trouble)* by helping anti-socials providing them shelter in his house.
78. He was ***born with a silver spoon in his mouth*** *(born in wealth and luxury)*.

Study the Idioms & their meanings, begins with 'C':

79. His honesty cannot be ***called in question*** *(dispute the truth of a statement)*.
80. Do not ***call a person by names*** *(abuse someone)*.
81. His conduct should be ***called to account*** *(ask one to answer for one's misconduct)*.
82. Now Prabir is simply ***coining money*** *(earning large sum of money)*.
83. Everybody should ***call a spade a spade*** *(to speak frankly, plainly)*.
84. The secret behind the matter has at last ***come to light*** *(publish)*.
85. Mr. Dey is ***coming to the front*** *(attain prominence)* in politics.

86. The boy has ***cut a sorry figure*** *(make a poor result in any action or in exam)* in the final examination.
87. He ***changed color*** *(become shocked and turned pale)* when I asked him about his result in the examination.
88. Shiba joined the contest and ***carried the day*** *(succeed in a contest)*.
89. I can't ***call to mind*** *(recollect)* the girl's name.
90. It is raining ***cats and dogs*** *(pouring heavily)* for two days.
91. His words ***cut her to the quick*** *(hurt one's feeling)*.
92. Tenida, one of Narayan Gangapadhyay's characters, used to tell ***cock and bull stories*** *(nonsense and absurd stories)*.
93. She came to me shed ***crocodile tears*** *(show of insincere sorrow through tears)* at my father's death.
94. Della was ***carried off her feet*** *(be wild with excitement)* when she discovered a proper gift for Jim.
95. His thesis contained ***chapter and verse*** *(full and precise reference to authority)* for the new theories he discussed therein.
96. By his skill in arguing he ***carried his point*** *(defeat the opponent in debate)*.
97. Employment is the ***crying need*** *(the essential)* of our youths to-day.

98. My scheme ***came to grief*** *(failed)* for want of fund.
99. You will ***come to grief*** *(be ruined)* if you follow that rogue.
100. The accountant of the company was charged with ***cooking the accounts*** *(prepare false accounts)*.
101. The prince became king when he ***came of age*** *(be adult)*.
102. Whatever he takes he ***carries all before him*** *(be completely successful)*.
103. Doing so, you only ***cutting your own throat*** *(ruin oneself)*.
104. He met me in the street and ***cut me dead*** *(make deliberate insult by ignoring)*.
105. The journalist ***cut him short*** *(to interrupt one)* in the middle of his confession.
106. The labor dispute in the company ***came to a head*** *(reached a crisis)* this week.
107. The police ***caught a Tarter*** *(encounter a person who prove to be stronger than the first)* in the man whom they arrested first.
108. In the contest he ***came off second-best*** *(is defeated)*.
109. He ***curries favor*** *(adopt mean ways to ingratiate oneself)* with his rich relatives.

Study the Idioms & their meanings, begins with 'D' & 'E':

110. Sanskrit is ***dead language*** *(a language out of use)* today when it should not be.
111. The soldier ***died game*** *(die fighting bravely)* against the enemy soldiers.
112. His father ***died in harness*** *(die while working)* and he was appointed in his place.
113. In the ***dead of night*** *(mid-hours of night)* Mr. Prime Minister declared the country is in emergency.
114. While telling you should ***draw the line*** *(fix the limit)* where to end.
115. The two statements ***do not hang together*** *(are not consistent with each other)*.
116. He is ***every inch*** *(entirely)* a miser fellow.
117. His every attempt to be a rich man ***ended in smoke*** *(failed)*.

Study the Idioms & their meanings, begins with 'F':

118. How a man of ***flesh and blood*** *(human nature)* can endure much than that.
119. His projects fell flat on the readers. His speech ***fell flat*** *(fail or have no effect)* on his hearers.

120. Many people in this vast world live ***from hand to mouth*** *(live without making any savings for future)*. If you have nothing to do, think about them.
121. He helped me many times in my need, I am thinking how to ***foot the bill*** *(to pay for it)*.
122. He left the service for good and engaged himself in writing novels.
123. Mr. Gupta ***falls foul of*** *(quarrel with)* everybody.
124. As he is a humbug, everybody ***fights shy of*** *(avoid from dislikes)* him.
125. This year the crop has ***fallen short of the expectations*** *(can't meet expectation)* of the farmer.
126. She was ***far and away*** *(very much)* the best of the singers who sang in the function.
127. His fame soon spread ***far and wide*** (**also:** far & near) *(everywhere)*

Study the Idioms & their meanings, begins with 'G':

128. The use of credit cards is ***gaining ground*** *(become more general and popular)* among the middle class.
129. Of late he is ***giving himself airs*** *(behave arrogantly)* with everybody.
130. He has ***got rid of*** *(be free of)* his unwelcome visitor.
131. He ***got the better of me*** *(overcome one)* at last.
132. He was guilty but ***got off easy*** *(get a light sentence or punishment)*.
133. He should not ***go back on*** *(fail to keep)* his word.
134. Boys ***give ears to*** *(listen to)* the lectures of the teacher attentively.
135. It will ***go hard with him*** *(prove a serious thing for one)* if he does not shun his evil company.
136. It ***went hard with us*** *(proved a serious thing for one)* to continue our studies when our father was dead.
137. She ***went out of her way*** *(take special effort and trouble)* to help the distressed.

138. Her simplicity ***goes to my heart*** *(touch one deeply)* then, and then her cruelty causes bloodshed.

139. This subject is ***Greek (or Hebrew)*** *(which could not be understood)* to me.
140. In need friends ***give you a cold shoulder*** *(treat one in cold manner)* is not a friend indeed.
141. Now-a-days, they are mostly biased ***giving a false coloring to*** *(misrepresent)* incidents; so, why to read them at all; and even read, why to believe them blindly.
142. She is ***great a hand at*** *(expert at)* organizing cultural programs.
143. He behavior ***give a handle to*** *(give a scope to)* suspicion.
144. A political leader should have the ***gift of the gab*** *(ability to talk fluently)*.

Study the Idioms & their meanings, begins with 'H':

145. Both of your arguments should not ***hang together*** *(be consistent)*.
146. Your argument will ***hold water*** *(unsound thing; unfit for scrutiny)* in the seminar.
147. You should try ***heart and soul*** *(with sincerity)* to solve the problem.
148. Anil is ***hand and glove*** *(very intimate)* with his friends.
149. A wife always ***hopes against hope*** *(hope for something in a critical moment, when it is difficult to manage)* is an eternal problem to some poor husbands to maintain their livelihood within limited income.
150. The women raised a ***hue and cry*** *(outcry or noise)* seeing the dacoits coming towards them.
151. He has ***hit the nail on the head*** *(say or do the right thing)* on this topic.
152. There is no ***hard and fast*** *(fixed)* rule in this matter.
153. This point will not ***hold good*** *(be applied)* in this discussion.

154. I believe that he ***has a hand in*** *(is concerned)* this matter.
155. I am tiring of hearing her ***harp on the same string*** *(dwell tediously on the same subject)*.
156. Becoming ***hard of hearing*** *(somewhat deaf)* in danger of others is one of the common social diseases.
157. People generally become ***hard of hearing*** *(somewhat deaf)* in old age.
158. As a politician he was ***head and shoulders*** *(very much)* above his contemporaries.
159. When he delivers lectures the listeners ***hang on their lips*** *(listened eagerly)*.

160. The dishonest businessmen should be dealt with severely, but the Govt. ***hangs fire*** *(hesitate)* to do so.
161. Our fate ***hung in the balance*** *(not decided)*.
162. He may be a handicapped boy, but his ***heart is in the right place*** *(faithful & true-hearted)*.

Study the Idioms & their meanings, begins with 'I':

163. The minister carried out the project ***in the teeth of*** *(in defiance of)* opposition.
164. She took my advice ***in good part*** *(without offence)*.
165. I am ***in a fix*** *(in a trouble situation)* and unable to take a decision.
166. ***In fine*** *(in the conclusion)* he uttered the key point of his discussion.
167. Diligence is sure to be rewarded ***in the long run*** *(ultimately)*.
168. He jumped out of the running bus ***in the nick of time*** *(just at the right moment)*.
169. The Police Inspector investigate the ***ins and outs*** *(full details of anything)* of the case.
170. He spent much time to probe into the matter and lost a pretty sum of money ***into the bargain*** *(in addition)*.
171. She told me that her son had got ***into hot water*** *(into trouble)*.
172. He described the event ***in a nutshell*** *(in brief)*.
173. He tried ***in vain*** *(fruitless)* to pass the examination.
174. He did the work ***in high spirits*** *(joyful)*.
175. The color of the screen of TVs are ***in character*** *(similar)* with that of Windows.
176. The boy is ***in the good books of*** *(favorite with)* the class-teacher.

177. That girl is ***in the bad books of*** *(not favorite with)* her teachers in the college.
178. The patients should not keep the doctor ***in the dark*** *(in ignorance)* of his or her illness.
179. The game will again start at 6p.m., and the players ***in the meantime*** *(between the time)* practice a little.
180. The police officer informed that the troubled situation is ***in hand*** *(under control)*.
181. A spirit of unrest is ***in the air*** *(found everywhere)* of the house.

182. The rogue murdered the man ***in cold blood*** *(deliberately and without a passion)*.
183. The police requested him to register his complaint ***in black and white*** *(in writing)*.
184. Everybody says that his business is ***in the running*** *(good prospect in a competition)*.
185. The preparation for election is going ***in full swing*** *(in full energy)*.
186. Since marriage you are ***in bad odor*** *(in bad repute)* with my relatives.
187. She seems to be ***ill at ease*** *(uneasy)* now and then.
188. I repaid his insult ***in kind*** *(in the same way)*.
189. Every man remains ***in a state of nature*** *(nakedly)* at the time of birth.

Study the Idioms & their meanings, begins with 'K':

190. He always keeps in touch with his ***kith and kin*** *(friends and relatives)*.
191. You cannot ***keep pace*** *(progress at equal rate)* with me though you may try very hard. It is called 'intelligence'.
192. He reads science journals regular and ***keep in touch with*** *(possess the intimate knowledge of)* the latest development.
193. The quarrelsome woman ***kicked up a row*** *(make great noise)* again and hit her son violently this time to knock him down.
194. I find you ***know a thing or two*** *(be wise or cunning)*.
195. Every time I go, she ***keeps a good table*** *(provide food luxuriously)*. Yet I don't know is it her love or other.
196. My poor father ***kept up appearances*** *(keep up an upward show, but condition is opposite)*, though earned nothing ocean, and he died a king.
197. I was unable to ***keep the wolf from the door*** *(keep off starvation)* and I took fasting every time during the Shibaratri.
198. You can trust him; he ***knows what's what*** *(know the ways of life, experienced)*.

Study the Idioms & their meanings, begins with 'L':

199. The new accountant of the office ***leaves no stone unturned*** *(use all available ways)* to satisfy his superiors.
200. The leader of the thieves took the ***lion's share*** *(the major portion)* of the booty.
201. Ram, a poet, felt ***like a fish out of water*** *(in a strange situation)* when he was to assist a businessman.

202. It is heard that some ruffians ***laid hands on*** *(attack and insult)* Peter when he was returning from the seminar.
203. In India under the British rule some people always tried to satisfy the British rulers for ***loaves and fishes*** *(material benefits)*.
204. Relatives ***left*** the young boy and his mother ***in the lurch*** *(leave into difficulties)* when his father died.

Study the Idioms & their meanings, begins with 'M':

205. People gathered in large number to hear his ***maiden speech*** *(first lecture)*.
206. Rabindranath Tagore ***made his mark*** *(make oneself distinguished)* at an early age.
207. He ***made up his mind*** *(decided)* to enter into business leaving his job with bank.
208. He ***makes a clean breast of*** *(confess frankly)* the unfair matter he was connected with.
209. The whole plan proved to be a ***mare's nest*** *(a false belief, a worthless thing)*.
210. The boy ***made light of*** *(treat lightly)* the teacher's warning.
211. The businessman ***makes the most of*** *(make the best advantage of)* the opportunity to expand his business.
212. I am sure the boy ***means business*** *(is eager)*.
213. The horror film ***makes the girl's blood creep*** *(make one horrified)*.
214. He ***moves heaven and earth*** *(makes every possible effort)* to have a good job.
215. During war or such like emergency there are always some people ***make a pile*** *(make a fortune)* taking advantage of the situation.

Study the Idioms & their meanings, begins with 'N':

216. He will prove himself to be ***not worth his salt*** *(quite worthless)* if he fails in the examination this year also.
217. He is ***not worth his salt*** *(quite worthless)* if he fails at this juncture.
218. He visits my house now and then.
219. The singer is ***not in voice*** *(not able to sing)* because of cough.

220. The law of capital punishment has now become ***null and void*** *(of no validity)* in most of the advanced countries.
221. All their efforts were ***nipped in the bud*** *(destroy at the root)* owing to lack of fund.
222. I could understand ***neither head nor tail*** *(nothing)* of the subject.
223. This type of job is ***not in my line*** *(out of my knowledge or sphere of action)*.

Study the Idioms & their meanings, begins with 'O':

224. His present action is not ***of a piece with*** *(pouring heavily)* his past actions.
225. This is ***of a piece with*** *(in keeping with)* the rest of his conduct.
226. She has been working ***on and off*** *(at intervals)* five years with this project.
227. She comes here ***off and on*** *(now and then)*.
228. The guards were ***on the alert*** *(on vigilant)*.
229. This custom is now ***out of date*** *(gone out of use)*.
230. A political leader often delivers his speech ***out of hand*** *(extempore)*. The boy has become ***out of hand*** *(out of control)* of his father.
231. The boys are ***out of spirits*** *(sad)* having no job.
232. I see, his behavior is really ***out of the way*** *(strange or abnormal)*. She went ***out of the way*** *(took special effort difficult for her)* to help me.
233. He says he feels ***out of sorts*** *(ailing, sick)*.
234. Chandan, my friend, has poetry ***on the brain*** *(rest constantly in one's thoughts)*.
235. Democracy soon to be ***on its last legs*** *(reaching the verge of ruin)* everywhere in the world due to the extreme corruption from its head to tail.
236. There was a time I was, Peter was ***over head and ears*** *(entirely)* in debt.

237. His popularity is ***on the wane*** *(decreasing)*.
238. He is ***out and out*** *(completely)* a rogue.
239. ***On the whole*** *(after all)* the book is well-written.
240. The deal left him thousands of rupees ***out of pocket*** *(being a loser)*.
241. The meal we took in an inn in the last summer was ***of a kind*** *(of a bad kind)*.
242. It is unwise to do anything ***on the spur of the moments*** *(without deliberation)*.

243. The growing mistrust and hatred among the nations show that another great war is ***on the cards*** *(not unlikely)*.
244. She is ***on the wrong side*** *(more than)* of thirty.
245. The unsettled case of land-dispute keeps the man ***on tenterhooks*** *(in a state of anxiety)*.

Study the Idioms & their meanings, begins with 'P':

246. Do not trust a man who ***plays fast and loose*** *(say one and do another thing)*.
247. The police examined the ***pros and cons*** *(in details)* of the murder case.
248. Discipline is ***part and parcel*** *(an essential portion)* of a student's life.
249. I know Anil's nature is to ***put a spoke in other's wheel*** *(hinder one in the execution of one's plan)*.
250. This unexpected new difficulty ***put me on my mettle*** *(roused me to do my best).*
251. When it is a case of cheating, I ***put my foot down*** *(take a determined step)*, for it is now a growing habit in men.
252. You did right ***put me in mind*** *(remind)* once again to send him a mail.
253. All the members of the municipality ***put their heads together*** *(consult one another)* to discuss the problem of their locality is the good sign of democracy, which is now ***on the wane*** *(decreasing)* is the danger for democracy, extreme decrying and less co-operation.
254. I ***pay him back in his own coin*** *(treat one in the same way as he treats)* paying him not for the recharge one.
255. In return of my trust, he ***played me false*** *(deceived)*.
256. He ***puts*** his newly composed grammar book ***on the market*** *(put for sale)*.
257. Kumar ***put a good face on*** *(bear up with courage)* his defeat in the war.
258. He ***pins his faith to*** *(give full reliance upon)* women's right to education.
259. The major often do this mistake, they ***play with fire*** *(trifle with serious matters unknowingly)* and hurt the sentiments of the minority.

260. We love to speak benevolence, but hardly to ***put our hands in our pockets*** *(give money in charity)*.
261. He is a straightforward man who can ***put two and two together*** *(make a correct inference)*.
262. Please don't ***put the screw on*** *(give pressure to do something)* me, let me decide what I should do in this situation.
263. You will ***put your foot in it*** *(to make serious mistake)* if you do not appear in the examination.

Study the Idioms & their meanings, begins with '*R*':

264. Finally, he ***rose to the occasion*** *(make oneself ready for an important situation)* in conducting publication of his own book for that goal.
265. The people ***rose in arms*** *(rise against)* against the tyrannical ruler every time.
266. My appeal for correction of name has been put in ***red-tape*** *(hindrance to disposal of any matter due to bureaucratic method)*, only they didn't need any while their type-writer input wrong.
267. The 26th January is a ***red-letter day*** *(memorable day, holiday)* for all Indians.
268. The dacoits were caught in ***red-handed*** *(be caught in the time of committing crime)*.
269. The drivers of the distant-plying buses ***rest on their oars*** *(stop and have rest in the time of working)*.
270. The ministers of the country do not pay attention to the ***rank and file*** *(common undistinguished people)*, who send them to the cabinet.
271. He is the ***right-hand man*** *(most close and efficient assistant)* of his chief.
272. Try to ***read between the lines*** *(realize the significance of the writing)* of the passage for précis writing.
273. During his tour to the village, he ***rubbed shoulder*** *(come into close contact)* with the common people of the country.
274. The workers work ***round the clock*** *(the whole day)* and we have our buildings, shopping malls, etc.

Study the Idioms & their meanings, begins with 'S':

275. He is a ***slow coach*** *(a lazy person)* and so he cannot prosper in life.

276. As a social reformer, he ***set his face against*** *(sternly opposed)* the leading parties.
277. The manager ***sent him about his business*** *(dismiss authoritatively)* as he was lazy and disobedient.
278. He, being poor, has but one ***square meal*** *(full meal)* a day.
279. Be cautious during typing to avoid ***slip of the pen*** *(a slight careless mistake in writing)*.
280. Forgive her, ***slip of the tongue*** *(a slight careless mistake in speaking)* is her normal habit or disease. By heart, she is a great one.
281. Should he not be punished for his ***sharp practice*** *(dishonest dealings)*?
282. I ***shook the dust off my feet*** *(depart indignantly)* from the meeting as it seemed merely disgusting and intriguing against the head master.
283. A renowned novelist lives at a ***stone's throw*** *(a short distance)* of my house.
284. The people in the locality ***shook in their shoes*** *(tremble with apprehension)* seeing the army entering the village.
285. This ***speaks volume for*** *(be abundant evidence of)* his honesty and sincere attitude to his work.
286. Though in distress, ***stick to your colors*** *(remain steady and faithful to one's principle)*, my boys.
287. Vidyasagar ***stuck his chin out*** *(show firmness)* in the introduction of widow-marriage in Bengal.
288. Vidyasagar was bold enough to ***stick his neck out*** *(expose oneself to harsh criticism by acting or speaking boldly)* in working for widow-marriage in the country.
289. Vidyasagar ***stuck to his guns*** *(maintain one's position under attack* to make the society free from age-old illiteracy and superstitions.
290. Every student should ***steer clear of*** *(take care to avoid)* bad company and any sort of intoxication.
291. At this hour of crisis, it is no good ***splitting hairs*** *(quarreling over trifling points)*.
292. He has nothing to boast of, yet he is ***swollen-headed*** *(conceited)*.
293. He ***serves his time*** *(go through an apprenticeship)* in Kolkata Medical College and expects to be a complete doctor soon.

294. I ***showed my hand*** *(to disclose one's plan of action)* to him expecting his co-operation or at least encouragement but it happened other.
295. Don't trust one who doesn't ***stick at nothing*** *(unsteady or undetermined)*.
296. This occupation has ***stood me in good stead*** *(proved to be useful)*.
297. It ***stands to reason*** *(an undoubted fact)* that a rich person can seldom be a man of outstanding creative genius.
298. Now that I have lost all my power and money, he is ***showing his teeth*** *(in a threatening mood)*.
299. I ***smell a rat*** *(have reason to suspect)* in his uncalled-for beneficence.
300. On the approach of the villagers in groups the dacoits ***showed a clean pair of heels*** *(ran away)*.
301. She ***stood her ground*** *(remain undisturbed)* against all adverse situations.
302. His ***stars are in the ascendant*** *(fortune favors)*.
303. The news of death of popular leader ***spread like wild fire*** *(spread rapidly)*.
304. She ***strained every nerve*** *(make utmost effort)* to nourish her fatherless child.
305. ***Sitting on the fence*** *(be in between two opinions and hesitate which side to join)* is now a general trend of the politicians.
306. He dreams of ***setting the Ganges on fire*** *(do or hope a surprising thing)*.

Study the Idioms & their meanings, begins with *'T'*:

307. In spite of all his brag he had ***to eat humble pie*** *(to apologize humbly, to yield under humiliating circumstances)*.
308. Take care what you say! You will have ***to eat your words*** *(to retract your statements, to take back what you have said)*.
309. I am prepared ***to meet you half-way*** *(come to a compromise with you.)*
310. It is silly ***to meet trouble half-way*** *(i.e., to anticipate it; to worry about it before it comes)*.
311. The cost of living has increased so much that he finds it difficult ***to make both ends meet*** *(to live within his income)*.
312. He ***took exception to*** *(object to)* my remark the other day.
313. He wants ***to pay off old scores*** *(to take revenge)* and be satisfied.

314. A sentimental person ***takes*** everything) ***to heart*** *(be deeply affected)*.
315. At the leader's encouraging words, his followers ***took heart*** *(to take courage)*.
316. Seeing the police coming the thief ***took to his heels*** *(ran away)*.
317. The student was ***taken to task*** *(rebuke, scold)* for his misconduct to junior teachers.
318. Why do people ***turn a deaf ear to*** *(do not hear to)* a person in danger, just look to yourself you'll get your answer.
319. He has ***turned over a new leaf*** *(change the course for better life)* by publishing his own book.
320. He who stays by ***through thick and thin*** *(under all conditions)* is a real friend.
321. My colleagues ***throw cold water*** *(discourage showing indifference)* on my new plan publishing a new book on composition after the book on grammar.
322. You can ***turn your hand to*** *(undertake a new job)* any work that suit you better.
323. He ***turns*** his new deal ***to account*** *(make profit)*.
324. He was pacing ***to and from*** *(here and there)* in the room.
325. Unemployment, corruption is ***the order of the day*** *(the present state of thing)*.
326. He translated the Bengali passage into English ***to the letter*** *(to every detail)*.
327. We must fight ***tooth and nail*** *(with one's utmost power)* to eradicate illiteracy from our country.
328. The villagers voted in his favor ***to a man*** *(everybody without exception)*.
329. He ***turns up his nose*** *(show disdain)* at your property earned by unfair means.
330. He has ***too many irons in the fire*** *(engaged in many jobs at the same time)*, yet he proceeds steadily.
331. We need guards who are ***true to their salt*** *(faithful to the employer)*.
332. This dress suits her ***to a T*** *(correctly)*.
333. ***The long and the short of*** *(the whole subject in a few words)* what I want to say is that I shall not join you in your new business.

334. The new officer wants ***to take stock of*** *(to look at carefully)* the whole matter before starts the investigation.
335. The explorers ***took life in their hands*** *(face great risk)* at every step of their journey in the unknown region.
336. His friend ***took the wind out of his sails*** *(make one's action ineffective by anticipation)* in his work of publishing an English Grammar book.
337. The man, being unable to work, wants ***to rest on his laurels*** *(to retire)*.
338. He has ***made good the loss*** *(to compensate the loss)*.
339. I know ***the ins and outs*** *(full details)* of his present deplorable condition.
340. He has become rich and now ***takes thing easy*** *(do not labor)*.
341. Peter profited in the business ***taking a leaf out of his friend's book*** *(imitate one or profit by one's example)*.
342. While giving him punishment, you should ***take into account*** *(consider)* also his noble deeds.
343. This is ***the thing*** *(the proper thing)* you should attempt.
344. I ***tried my hand*** *(make an effort)* to write science fiction at late hours and I failed entire.
345. It is difficult for a poor man like Peter ***to keep his hand above water*** *(to keep out of debt)*.
346. Her manager was a wicked man ***to the backbone*** *(to the core)*.
347. He ***took away my breath*** *(to surprise one very much)* when he gave me news of his becoming gold medalist in doctorate.
348. Try your best ***to crow over*** *(to win over)* your opponent.
349. You should not expect me ***to see eye to eye*** *(in complete harmony)* with you in this work.
350. She is a habitual liar, so everybody ***takes*** her words ***with a grain of salt*** *(doubt)*.
351. This shoe fits you, madam, ***to a nicety*** *(exactly)*.
352. Don't ***thrust your nose into*** *(interfere unnecessarily)* anybody's affair.
353. He has ***two strings to his bow*** *(two sources of income to live on)* as he is working in a Govt. office and privately practicing in Homeopathy.
354. The patent has ***turned the corner*** *(pass over the crisis)*.
355. A he ***talks sharp*** *(talk about business only)*, nobody likes him.

Study the Idioms & their meanings, begins with *'U'* & *'W'*:

356. A business has its ***ups and down*** *(rise and fall)*.

357. I asked the shop-keeper to give me a dictionary book with meanings ***up-to-date*** *(to the present time)*.
358. Your performance was not ***up to the mark*** *(equal to the standard)*.
359. The book which he requires is ***under his nose*** *(at very close to one's presence)*, but being absentminded he cannot see it.
360. The lecture hall is filled ***up to the eyes*** *(fully)*.

361. Consult with him; he is a person of ***well-balanced*** *(reasonable)* opinions.
362. My proposal was accepted ***with one voice*** *(unanimously)*.
363. A wearer knows ***where the shoe pinches*** *(where the trouble lies)*.
364. The king ruled his subjects ***with a high hand*** *(with oppression)*.
365. He did the job ***with might and main*** *(with the utmost strength)*.
366. He ***washes his hands of*** *(refuse to do anything more)* the whole matter.
367. I can accept your statement ***without reserve*** *(full)* if you add this point to it.
368. Gandhiji received Louis Fischer in his Ashram ***with open arms*** *(with an open heart, warm welcome)*.
369. Sachin ***won his laurels*** *(acquire a distinction or glory)* in cricket.
370. She ***won her spurs*** *(acquire one's reputation)* as a pop singer.
371. The Indian Railway soon to become a ***white elephant*** *(a costly unprofitable object)* to the Govt. after the Indian Airlines.
372. At the battle of Marengo, Napoleon was ***within an ace of*** *(on the point of)* defeat. (i.e., he was very nearly defeated.)

5. Detail study: Clause & its Kinds

Like a phrase, a clause is also named after its roles or functions in a sentence. Based upon clauses, the classification of sentences (according to structure) also depends.

30. What is a clause?

➤ A group of words, with a unit of finite verb and subject, that forms a part of a sentence is called a **Clause**. Unlike a phrase, a clause conveys a thought or an idea of the speaker. Study the chart:

A Phrase	A Clause
1) A phrase consists of a group of words.	1) A clause also consists of a group of words.
2) A phrase does not have a subject & a predicate;	2) A clause must have a subject & a predicate (i.e., a finite verb);
3) A phrase forms a meaning, like a single word, may be some broad;	3) A clause conveys a sense or a thought, complete or incomplete;
4) It is a smaller unit of language, comparatively smaller than a clause.	4) It is also a unit of language, comparatively larger than a phrase.

31. For example:

- *As he is ill*, he cannot come.
- This is the boy *who did it*.

- If we count finite verbs, we have two in each of them that means, here, each sentence consists of two clauses.
- The clauses in sentence-1, are— '**he cannot come**', '***As he is ill***' &
- In sentence-2, the clauses are— '**This is the boy**', '***who did it.***'

How to find clauses in a sentence

32. As said, *by count of finite verb units* (two or more together, like main verb with its auxiliaries must to be considered as one unit of finite verb, as are found in different tenses). Then, subjects, objects, others, are to be considered to be an entire clause. For illustration, read the followings:

- Nikky is not a stupid boy.
- You are a boy and I am a girl.
- Madhuri Dixit who is an actress won the prize.

- If we count the number of finite verbs in the sentences they have:
  - The sentence 1 has only one finite verb is equal to (=) It has one clause. The sentence is **Simple Sentence.**
  - The sentence 2 and 3, both have two unit of finite verbs each = they have two clauses each;
  - When a co-ordinate conjunction **'and'** is used in the 2nd sentence, we have used the sub-ordinate conjunction **'who'** in sentence no- 3.
  - Thus, the 2nd sentence is a **Compound Sentence** while the third sentence is a **Complex Sentence**, based on the nature of clauses used (i.e., defined by what kind of conjunctions have been used in them, in the clauses and how do they role in the sentence.)
  - So, often we see one thing is influenced by some other, by certain other things used in or used as.

- ***So, to define number of clauses:***

- **Points to be remembered:** Finite verb is the main indication of a clause; either it is of a Principal, Sub-ordinate or Co-ordinate clause. **Every clause must have a finite verb** *or a finite verb group* (i.e., helping + main verb to be considered only as one unit of finite verb) i.e.**,**

- **one finite verb / one-unit of finite verb = one clause,** (along with their subject, object or others.)

Kinds of Clauses

33. According to function or use, clauses are of the following three kinds. They are:

A. **Principal** or **Independent Clause,**
B. **Co-ordinate Clause** (where the clauses are of equal rank, linked by a Co-ordinate Conjunction)

C. **Subordinate** or **Dependent Clause** (where the clauses are depended on a principal, and linked by a Sub-ordinate Conjunction)

- Based on Clauses, Sentences are also of three kinds: (This division of sentences, we call, is 'According to Structure'.)
  - A) **Simple** Sentence (with *only one principal clause*),
  - B) **Compound** Sentence (*principal + co-ordinate clause*)
  - C) **Complex** Sentence (*principal + at least 1 sub-ordinate clause*)

A. Principal Clause

34. The clause which can stand by itself as a complete & separate sentence without depend on any other part but other may depend on it, is called the **Principal Clause**.

A Principal Clause by itself also can form independent sentences. Study the examples:

1) I shook my head.
2) I won't let you down.
3) I'll do something.
4) I came to the living room at midnight.
5) I will the Allahabad University and repeat from there.
6) I wished (that) he would figure out (that) I wanted to cry.
7) Baba looked like (as if) I had stabbed him.

All the underlined are the example of Principal Clauses or Simple Sentences.

B. Co-ordinate Clause

35. Read the sentences & find out Co-Ordinate Clause:

1) I went to Kolkata *and then left for Delhi*.
2) He does not know me *but I seek help from him*.

- In the first sentence the **verbs**— 'went' & 'left' have a common subject— 'I'.

So, there are two clauses respectively– "I went to Kolkata" & *"then I left for Delhi"*—& they can stand by themselves as two complete sentences, as:

a) I went to Kolkata.
b) Then, I left for Delhi.

Both are independent & of equal rank. Thus, they both are the Principal Clauses. However, the later (2nd main or principal) when connected with **'and'**, the clause become a co-ordinate clause. In the sentence, the conjunction, **'and'** is an example of Cumulative Co-ordinate Conjunction that joins two clauses of equal rank.

- In the 2nd sentence the **verbs**— 'know' & 'seek' have two different subjects— **'He'** & **'I'**.

And here the two clauses are– "He does not know me" & *"I seek help from him"*. They are both independent, as they can stand by themselves as two different sentences; as,

a) He does not know me.
b) I seek help from him.

Here too, the two Principal Clauses are connected by a co-ordinate conjunction **'but'** which is Adversative or express a contrast idea (another kind of Co-ordinate Conjunction) and thus, here too the sentence is a **Compound Sentence.**

Definition

The principal clause which is directly linked with a co-ordinate conjunction is named after it, as **Co-ordinate clause,** when the other is left to call as the **Principal Clause** in the sentence.

If we again read the above sentences in this way-

- I went to Kolkata
- *...and then left for Delhi.*

- and

- He does not know me
- *...but I seek help from him.*

The italic and bold clauses— '*and then left for Delhi*', '*but I seek help from him*'—are two examples of **Co-Ordinate Clauses.**

Note: To understand 'Co-ordinate clause better, study well the chapter of Conjunctions and its classification.

36. Some examples of **Co-Ordinate Conjunctions are:** *and, but, yet, or, not only...but also, either...or, neither...nor, therefore,* etc. Study them in the sentences and note their roles.

Kinds of Co-ordinate Clauses

37. The division of Co-ordinate Clause depends on the kinds of Co-ordinate Conjunctions. In other words, we can say, the division depends on the functions of Co-ordinate Conjuncts which are as the following:

Functions of Co-ordinate conjuncts

13

Cumulative	• **That simply joins two words, phrases, clauses of equal rank of action or names.** • and, also, too, as well as, both—and, not only—but also, etc.
Alternative	• **That refers selection between two.** • Either...or, neither...nor, whether, or, else etc.
Adversative	• **The conjunctions that show contrast.** • still, yet, only, but, however, nevertheless, though–yet, etc.
Illative	• **Which express aninference (that refersto come conclusion or to last decision.)** • Therefore, for, so, then, so then etc.

➢ Cumulative Co-ordinate Clause:

- We carved not a line, ***and*** we raised not a stone.
- God made the country ***and*** man, made the town.
- Vishal & Virat are good bowlers. (Vishal is a good bowler & Virat is a good bowler.)
- **Note:** If such conjunctions are used to refer a single object or a subject; i.e., a single thing, it is better to treat as a simple sentence, but not as a compound; as the following:

- Two ***and*** two make four. (***Here:*** the two and two make only one number that is four; which is not possible without the other.)
- Bread ***and*** milk is a wholesome food. (It is also an example of simple sentence. The food is made of the two 'bread and milk', but not possible without the other.)

➢ Alternative Co-ordinate Clause:

- She must weep, ***or*** she will die.
- ***Either*** he is mad, ***or*** he feigns madness.
- Is that story true ***or*** false? (Is that story true or is that story false?)
- ***Neither*** a borrower, ***nor*** a lender be.
- We can travel by land ***or*** water. (We can travel by land, or we can travel by water.)
- They toil not, ***neither*** do they spin.
- ***Either*** you are mistaken, ***or*** I am.
- Walk quickly, ***else*** you will not overtake him.

➢ Adversative Co-ordinate Clause:

- Our hoard is little, ***but*** our hearts are great.
- The man is poor, ***but*** honest. (The man is poor, but he is honest.)
- He is slow, ***but*** he is sure.
- I was annoyed, ***still*** I kept quiet.
- I would come; ***only*** that I am engaged.
- He was all right; ***only*** he was fatigued.

➢ Illative Co-ordinate Clause:

- Something certainly fell in; ***for*** I heard a splash.
- All precautions must have been neglected, ***for*** the plague spread rapidly.

38. Study more Co-ordinate Clauses. Try to find out their types:

- Loaf about less on Sundays **and** you will be without a headache on Monday.
- He put it in an envelope **and** (he) sealed it.
- Father snatched the letter away from Swami **and** (he [the father]) tore it up.

- It required no vehicle except his own body **and** (it) cost him nothing but his energy.
- We just had to make the most of each other **and** we did.
- We started out, **and** up went the kite like a bird.
- I tripped **and** fell over the rocks.

C. Sub-ordinate Clause

39. Read the following sentence and find out Sub-ordinate Clause:

*As he **is** ill*, he cannot **come.**

➢ **'is' & 'come'**—both are the Finite verbs. '**is**' is a primary auxiliary used as main verb in the sentence.

So, the sentence has two clauses.

The clauses are: As he is ill, & ... he cannot come.

➢ Now the question is what kind they are? (According to the completion of sense)

- **As he is ill ...**

- The part, obviously, not telling us a complete sense; as it depends on something, other part of the statement; and the clause is linked by a Sub-ordinate Conjunction **'as'**;

- As "**As he is ill**" can't stand by itself; can't make the sense complete; so, it is a "**Sub-ordinate Clause**", while **'he cannot come'** is a **Principal** or **Main Clause**.

Definition

The clause that can't stand by itself, and which for completion of sense, **depends on the main clause**, is called the **Sub-ordinate Clause**. A sub-ordinate clause is essentially connected with sub-ordinate conjunctions. Some of sub-ordinate conjunctions are as the followings:

- *Before, after, because, that, than, if, whether, though, although, till, unless, as, when, where, while, why, how,* etc.

➢ **A Sub-ordinate** clause is also known as '**Dependent**', '**Nonessential**' or '**Nonrestrictive**' clause by different grammarians.

40. Let's have a glance of Sub-ordinate Conjunctions **which form Sub-ordinate Clause. Study the conjunctions that do function like an adverb:**

Adverbial function of conjunction	Sub-ordinate conjunctions
TIME	**after, before, since, as soon as, while, until, as, so long as, till.**
PURPOSE	**in order that, lest, so that, that.**
CAUSE	**because, since, as.**
CONDITION	**provided, supposing, unless, as, if, whether.**
RESULT/EFFECT	**so...that**
COMPARISON	**that, as...as**
CONTRAST	**though, although, however, even if.**

The above examples of adverbial functions of conjunction you will study through the following three kinds of sub-ordinate clauses.

Kinds of Sub-ordinate Clauses

41. Examine the following sentences. First, underline the finite verbs:

a) I expect ***that*** I shall get a prize.
b) The umbrella ***which*** has a yellow handle is mine.
c) ***When*** I was younger I used to fly kites.
d) I remember the house ***where*** I was born.

- If we count Finite Verbs, we will get two in each of them in the above sentences (which are underlined), that means, each sentence has two clauses, which are joined by – ***'that', 'which', 'when', & 'where'.*** The words are the ***sub-ordinate conjunctions***, while the clauses in italic, are the examples of '**Sub-ordinate Clauses** to form each Complex Sentence in a, b, c, d serial number.

- Now the question is, 'what kind of sub-ordinate clauses they are?' **Please study the definitions in the following chart:**

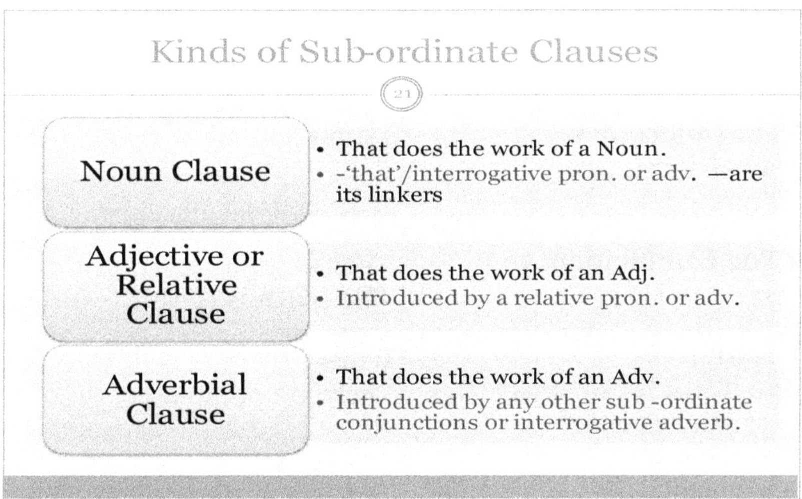

1. Noun Clause

- I expect ***that I shall get a prize***.

I expect... (**What** do you expect?)

Ans.: ...that I shall get a prize. = object to the verb 'expect'.

Subject+ verb + object

The complete sentence is consisted of **Subject+ verb + object**; of which the object ... **'that I shall get a prize'** itself is a clause & has done the function of a Noun. So, it is a **'Noun Clause'.**

- To know which are the Noun Clauses, study the functions of a Noun, first.

The Functions of Noun:

Nouns do the following functions. It is used-

1. As subject to the verb,
2. As object to the verb,

3. As object to a preposition,
4. As complement to the subject or object,
5. As phrase-in-apposition.

Function of Noun clause/As used	Examples
a) The subject of a verb	• *When he will come* is uncertain. • *Why my friend failed* is known to all.
b) The object of a verb	• I know *where he lives*. • She said *that she did not love me or anybody*.
c) The object of a preposition	• I know nothing of *what he will do*. • It depends on *how he behaves*.
d) The complement to a verb	• **That is** *what we expected*. • **The truth is** *he is ill.*
e) as noun in apposition [to give more information to either subject, object or complement]	• It *that he has come*, is true. • There is a rumor *that he is a dead*. • The news, that he is dead, is fake.

How to find a clause to be a **Noun**, or an **Adjective** or an **Adverb** is the best way to know the function or role of the clause in the sentence rather than knowing about different conjunctions (sub-ordinate), relative or interrogative pronoun or adverb, merely, though that helps a far.

Study the examples carefully, wherein all the sub-ordinate clauses are only the Noun Clauses. Study their functions:

1. I know *that he is ill*. [what do you know? = that he is ill. object to the verb]

2. They say *(that) he is ill*. [what do they say? = object to the verb. 'that' is understood.]

3. The truth is *he is ill*. [complement to the verb]

4. It, *that he is ill*, is true. [as noun in apposition]

5. *That he is ill* is known to all. [as subject of the verb]

6. I know *how ill he is*. /I know *how he is*. [what do you know? = the answer is 'object' to the verb 'know'. Though, 'how'-a relative adv., the clause is a Noun Clause]

7. I know *why he is ill*. ['why'- a relative adv., but the clause is again a Noun Clause. a answer to the question, 'what do you know? Answer is an object to the verb 'know']

8. I shall enquire *is he ill*. [without a connecting word but simply as a question. The clause is again a Noun Clause. what will you enquire?]

9. I shall enquire *if he is ill*. [this if clause is also a noun clause]

10. I shall enquire *who is ill*. ['who'-a relative pronoun, and the clause is again a noun clause.]

11. I ask him *if he is ill*. [the clause is a direct object; so, it is a a noun clause.]

12. I ask *if/whether he is ill*. [example of noun clause]

42. More Examples of Noun Clauses:

1) Swami knew how strict his father could be.
2) They said that even the headmaster is afraid of him.
3) This is what I want to tell you about.
4) He said it was all his fault.
5) Claude & I didn't understand what he meant.
6) Do you want to know what became of your kite?
7) *When he will come,* is uncertain.
8) *Why my friend failed* is known to all.
9) I know *where he lives*. That is *what we expected*.
10) She said *that she did not love me or anybody*.
11) I know nothing of *what he will do*.
12) It depends on *how he behaves*.

→ All the underlined are the examples of Noun Clauses.

2. *Adjective or Relative Clause*

- The umbrella ***which has a yellow handle,*** is mine.

Which umbrella is yours? = '*which has a yellow handle*'.

The clause describes its antecedent **Noun, 'umbrella'**, which is the subject of the main clause. So, the answer of the question (i.e., the sub-ordinate clause) does the function of an Adjective. So, it is an **Adjective or relative Clause.**

- I remember the house ***where I was born***.

Here again, the underlined sub-ordinate clause, ***where I was born***', describes its antecedent noun, 'the house'. So, here, the clause, again is an example of **Adjective** or **Relative Clause**.

- **Study the Functions of Adjectives to know an adjective clause better:**

- An Adjective describes a noun or a pronoun. It describes:
  a) To say of good or bad qualities;
  b) To say of number (quantity);
  c) To say of measurement, if any, etc. of a Noun or Noun Equivalent word or words in the sentences.

- Find out similarities of the functions of **Adjectives Clauses** with the functions of **adjectives in the sentences**:
  1) I know the **boy** who did it.
  2) He was a brilliant **player** who did a hat trick taking wickets in the last series.
  3) This is the **place** where I was born.
  4) Do you know the **reason** why he failed in the Exam?
  5) I have lost the **book** (which) you gave me.
  6) That is the **man** (whom) I saw.
  7) The **book** (which) he bought has been lost.

8) I have forgotten **the story** (that) he told me.
9) You can see **the cat** as he really is.

In all the above sentences, the **underlined sub-ordinate clauses describe their antecedent nouns in bold**. And thus, all the sub-ordinate clauses here, are the examples of **adjective** or **relative clause.**

- **Comparative study of Noun clause & Adj. clause**

➢ *Noun Clauses*	➢ *Adjective Clause*
a) Tell me *who did it*. b) Tell me *when he will come*. c) Tell me *why you have done this*. d) I know *how he did it*.	a) Tell me about the **person** *who did it*. b) Tell me the **time** *when he will come*. c) Tell me the **reason** *why you have done this*. d) I know the **way** *how he did it*.

3. *Adverbial Clause*

- *When I was younger,* I used to fly kites.

'When I was younger', the clause denotes a time of 'when I used to fly kites.

When did you use to fly kites? **Ans.: 'When I was younger'**. The answer to the question denotes the time of an action, so it is an **Adverbial Clause.**

The above-mentioned clause depends on main for its sense to complete, so, the clause is also termed as the **Dependent** or **Sub-ordinate Adverbial Clause**, and
'**I used to fly kites**'—is the **Principal Clause** in the sentence.

❑ For better understand an adverbial clause, we need to study the **Functions of Adverbs**:

⌘ An Adverb do the following functions, **add meaning** to a **verb**, **an adjective** or **an adverb**, etc.
- It mentions a **time**;
- Tells about **place** where something happens;

- Referring a cause or **reason**;
- Telling about result or **effect** of an action;
- Referring **condition**, **purpose** or **manner**;
- Tells of **concession**, **compare** or **contrast**;
- States a **frequency** of an action, etc.

43. Study the following chart how the adverbial clauses are:

Function as:	Examples
a) Indicate time	1. Wait *until I come*, 2. He came *when I was there*. 3. Strike *while the iron is hot*. 4. He came *after I had left*. 5. I went out *before he arrives*. 6. Go on your task *till it is finished*. 7. *As* he entered the school gate, an idea occurred to him.
b) Indicate place	1. Stay *where you are*. 2. Return *whence you come*. 3. I am able to find out *wherever you go*. 4. Go *wherever you like* to. 5. She went out *you know the place*. 6. Start from *where you finished last day*.
c) Indicate cause or reason	• I could not come *because I was ill*. • *As I was ill,* I could not come. • *Since I am ill,* you'll lead the party. • I am sorry *that you said this*.
d) Indicate result	• What have I done *that you desert me*? • I am so tired *that I cannot walk*. • He is such a fool *that I cannot depend on him*.
e) Indicate manner	• Travel *as you like*. • It happened *as I expected*. • I'm not sure *how it happened*.

f) Indicate purpose	• We read *that we may learn*. • He works hard *in order that/so that he may succeed.* • Walk slowly *lest you should fall*.
g) Indicate condition or supposition (if clause)	• *If I succeed,* I shall help you. • I shall not go *unless you come*. • I may come *in case I have time*.
h) Indicate concession or contrast	1. *Though he is poor*, he is honest. 2. *Even if I fail*, I shall not give up hope. 3. *Although they were present*, they said nothing. 4. *However, you strong may be*, I am not afraid of you. 5. *Whatever you may say*, I do not believe you. 6. *Whoever he may be*, he cannot be allowed.
i) Indicate comparison or degree	• He is not so tall *as his brother is.* • He is as wise *as you are*. • She is taller *than you are*.
j) Indicate frequency	• I visit to the cinema hall *whenever a good film is shown.* • She comes always *when I visit the town.*

44. Compare clauses as Noun & Adverb; table-1:

As Noun Clause	***As Adverbial Clause***
• I am sure of you will succeed. (Object of preposition) • He is satisfied of that you are right. (Object of preposition)	• I am sure you will succeed, as you are a brilliant. (Refers to cause] • He is satisfied that you are right. (Refers a cause of his being satisfied.)

• Be careful of what you say. (Object of preposition)	• Be careful what you say as you are a direct speaker. (refers cause of his being 'careful'.)

45. Compare Clauses as Adjective & Adverb; table-2:

➢ ***As Adjective Clause***	➢ ***As Adverbial Clause***
• My **brother** *who is ill* cannot come. • The **picture** *which was spoiled* has been thrown away. • I shall send my **brother** *who will do the work*. ➢ Each one describes its antecedent nouns, in bold.	• My brother cannot come, *because he is ill*. • The picture has been thrown away *because it was spoiled*. • I shall send my brother *that he may do the work*. ➢ First two refers 'cause', while the 3rd refers to 'purpose'.

46. We can convert a clause to another in most cases:

- The **type of a clause (sub-ordinate) depends upon the work done by it**, but **not on linking words solely**.
- Based on its work, role or function, a clause may be **a Noun, Adjective or Adverbia**l. Study the chart:

43

A sentence in different clauses:

The **type of a clause depends upon the work done by it**, but not on linking words.

That's why a clause may be **a Noun/ Adjective /Adverbial** clause.

I know *where he lives*.	**Noun clause**, **(object of 'know' by question —what do you know?)**
I know the place *where he lives*.	**Adjective clause**, **(qualifying or describing the 'place' by question—which place?)**
I shall go *where he lives*.	**Adverbial clause**, **(add meaning to the verb 'shall go' -by question —where? Where will you go?)**

Conditionals (if clause) -Meaning & Explanation

47. The term **'conditional'** literally means '***depending on something***'; as,

'Payment is conditional upon delivery of the goods.'

- *What does the above sentence mean?*

= **If the goods are not delivered, the money will not be paid.**

- The same thing happens to a conditional clause or sentence, where **the impact of the main clause is conditioned on the dependent clause**, i.e., 'one action (the action of main clause) will not happen unless the other (the action of the dependent or 'if' clause) i.e., it also means the main clause of such sentence is not entirely independent, it is a but a bit different from other principal or main clauses with their Sub-Ordinate Adverbials.

- *The Conditionals generally begin with **'if'**, but also sometimes with **'unless'**, **'when'** or any other word with the verb form that express the condition of* '**possibilities or 'certainty'** *of an action* *or state (i.e., something must happen or be true, if another thing is to happen or be true.'); as,*

→ If I were a bird, I had two wings.
→ If I had wife, she should cook me delicious food.
→ If it rains, the picnic will be cancelled.
→ If you heat ice, it melts.

48. Read the chart of four Conditionals:

Conditionals

45

	If Clause	Main Clause
Zero Conditional: (facts, habits & scientific truths) ✓(present+present/ past+past)	oIf I wake up late, oWhen I woke up late, * Express certainty	I miss the bus. I missed the bus.
First Conditional: [likely future result of an present action] (present+future)	oIf I wakeup late, * Express possibility, real or unreal	I will miss the bus.
Second Conditional: [imaginary situations in the past about future; thinking of future standing in the past] (simple past+pastof future)	oIf I woke up late, * But I did not wake up late, & I did not miss the bus(unreal fact)	I would miss the bus.
Third Conditional: (imaginary situation in the past; same situation as of 2nd, using only in perfect tenses) (past perfect+ past of future perfect)	oIf I had wokeup late yesterday, * But I hadn't woke up late, and I didn't miss the bus. (unreal fact)	I would have miss the bus.

- There are **four kinds of Conditional Sentences** in English. They are as the above shown in the chart and in the following read their illustrations and examples more in sentences:

A. **Zero Conditional:** While other three conditional sentences express 'possibility', real or unreal, Zero Conditional is used to express '**certainty**', i.e., <u>*talk about facts, habits & scientific truths*</u> that is ***always true, or was true*** in the past; as,
→ **If** you **mix** blue and red, you **get** purple.

→ **If** you **heat** ice, it **melts**.
→ **If** I **asked** her to come with us, she always **said,** 'No'.
→ **If** you **heat** water, it **boils.**
→ Water **boils if** you **heat** it.
→ **When** you **heat** ice, it **melts.**
→ Ice **melts when** you **heat** it.
→ **If** it **snows**, the grass **gets** white.
→ The grass **gets** white **if** it **snows**.
→ **When** it **rains**, the grass **gets** wet.
→ The grass **gets** wet **when** it **rains**.

Form: *Both the clauses (if clause & the main clause) are always in the same tense:* ***present*** *+* ***present*** *or* ***past*** *+* ***past****)*

B. **First Conditional:** express a possible situation in the future standing in the present. It predicts a likely result in the future of a present situation or action by 'if' clause; as,
→ **If I finish** my task this afternoon, I **will have** time to go the party tonight. (It is still morning and I can do it, because still I have enough time.)
→ **If** it **rains**, we **will stay** at home.
→ He **will arrive** late **unless** he **hurries** up.
→ Sophia **will buy** a new car, **if** she **increases** her savings.
→ **If** he **finishes** on time, we **will go** to the movies.
→ We **will go** to the movies **if** he **finishes** his work on time.

*(**If** or **the conditional clause** is in present tense, while the **main clause** is in future tense.)*

C. **Second Conditional:** used to talk about the consequences of a hypothetical action (***hypothetical***—*which are less likely to happen at present or in the future,* ***as time is left a little to complete the task*** (if you were a superman or others helped you, you probably could; but you are not a superman & not others helped you); as,
→ **If I finished** my task this afternoon, I **would have** time to go the party tonight. (In the current situation, it is now noon or early afternoon, a little chance to complete the task by the time.)
→ **If** I **were** a rich woman, I **would travel** around the world. (But I am a poor woman; it is the reality, and so, there is little probability to travel around the world.)

→ **If** I **weren't watching** TV, I **would be playing** tennis. (But time for both actions is now over.)
→ We **would go** to Paris this summer **if** we **passed** in all subjects. (As already we failed there is no chance to go to Paris.)
→ **If** I **were** an alien, I **would be** able to travel around the universe. (But am I? No, so I can't travel like an alien.)

*(**If clause** simple past, while the **main clause** is in conditional past, i.e., past of future, e.g., verb with '**would**' or '**should**' as past form of will or shall & the base verb)*

D. **Third Conditional:** used to talk about ***an imaginary situation in the past*** *that had not happened, so its consequences are also impossible to happen or did not happen*; as,
→ **If** you **had studied**, you **would have passed** the examination.
→ **If** I **hadn't been** sick, I **would have gone** to your party.
→ **If** I **had finished** my task this afternoon, I **would have had** time to go to the party tonight. (Now impossible)
→ **If** I **had travelled** to Italy, I **would have visited** Luca. (*But I had not travelled to Italy and, therefore, I did not visit Luca.)*
→ **If** you **had got** a good mark, **would you have complained** to the teacher? (*But your mark was bad, so we don't know for sure what you would have done.)*
→ What **would you have done** if it **had snowed** last weekend? (*But it didn't snow.)*

*(**If clause** past perfect, while the **main clause** is in conditional past perfect, i.e., past of future perfect, e.g., verb with '**would have**' or '**should have**' as past form of will have or shall have)*

49. The Conditional Tense of Modals:

- With the help of ***'shall'*** & ***'will',*** we form Future Tense. When a future tense is used for reporting, they often changed into past of future, 'will' & 'shall' are turned to **'would'** or **'should'** (and thus some other modals too, like 'can' to 'could', 'may' to 'might', 'must'/ 'have to' to 'had to', etc.)

- This change of form from Future to Past Future of the Modal Verbs is known as **Conditional Tense** of shall or will or **Conditional Tense** of **Modals**. Thus, we have four conditional forms of shall or will. They are:

(A) **Simple Conditional:** (would/should + base verb); as,

→ He ***said*** that he ***would go*** there soon.
→ I ***told*** her that I ***would write*** for her.
→ Peter ***said*** that he ***would write*** a book on composition soon.

(B) **Progressive Conditional:** (would/should + be+ -ing form of base verb)

→ I told him that I ***would/should be writing***.
→ She said that she ***would be waiting*** for me forever.
→ They said that they ***would be waiting*** for us there.

(C) **Perfect Conditional** &: (would/should + have+ 3rd form of base verb)

→ He said that the train ***would have left*** before they arrived the station.
→ Priya said that I ***would have gone*** before she reached there at the bus-stop.
→ Jubinal assured us that the train ***would have left*** the station before the blast occurred.

(D) **Perfect Progressive Conditional:** (would/should + have been + -ing form of base verb)

→ He said that he ***would have been dancing*** after it began.
→ Kanchan said that he ***would have been performing*** even after he reached nineteen.
→ She ***would have been singing*** till it was declared over.

> **Note:** Generally, **'if', 'unless', 'when' clauses** are known as **Conditional Clause** & the above are known as **Conditional past of Modals**.

50. Sometimes, introducing conjunctions **'if', 'unless'** or **'when'** which determine or denote Conditionals, are sometimes left understood or omitted in the sentences; as,

- **Had I been** *(If I had been)* rich, I would help you.

- **Were I** *(If I were)* present, I would oppose you?
- ***I succeed*** (*If I succeed*), I shall help you.
- You have not come, I shall not go,
  =(I shall not go ***unless*** you come.)
- I have time, I may come in.
  =I may come in; ***in case*** I have time.
- He gets leave, sure he will come.
  =He will come ***provided*** he gets leave.
- I succeed or not, I shall try.
  =I shall try, ***whether*** I succeed or not.

51. Exercise (identify what kind of conditional, used):

1) If you do not win scholarship, your father will be very sad.
2) If I have enough strawberries, I will bake a strawberry cake for you.
3) If you don't brush your teeth regularly, your teeth decays.
4) If she had found his phone number, she might have called him for the party.
5) If I could have spoken English very well, I would have talked to the tourists from London.
6) I wouldn't have called if I had known that she wasn't at home.
7) If I won the lottery, I would travel a lot.
8) If they sold the land, they would be rich.
9) If it rains, we will cancel the trip.
10) If you study, you'll pass the exam.
11) If you throw salt to the water, it boils later.
12) If I were you, I wouldn't drink anymore?
13) If I understood what the teacher said, I could tell you.
14) If she had gone on a picnic, she would have had a lot of fun.

WISH CLAUSE

52. The **Wish Clauses—are often <u>Noun clauses</u>** <u>(with or without</u> <u>**'that'**,</u> & <u>**Adverbial clauses** (with the linker **'if'**</u>).

In sentence, 'wish clause' appear to be another principal clause (**when they are noun clause actually**) as sub-ordinate conjunction 'that' remains omitted here and sometimes the principal clause too; & with **'if'** they are often Adverbial clauses.

A 'wish clause' can be used in three sets or forms or in tense; as,

(A) **Wish + Past Tense of the verbs** (here, the wish is about 'Now' of Present time); as,

(1) I wish I could see it.
(2) I wish she weren't here.
(3) I wish Rossie knew the answer.
(4) I wish you had more money to lend.
(5) I wish you had a heart to know me better.
(6) If I were a bird! (The principal clause is omitted here; if she were a bird, she would do something; what? The listener knows well.)
(7) We wish she could see it.
(8) We wish Martin weren't there.
(9) Paul wishes he weren't here among us.
(10) Poulomi wishes if she had wings.
(11) Poulomi wishes if they had a car.
(12) They wish if they had jobs.

(B) **Wish + Past Perfect Tense of the verbs** (here, the wish is about 'then' of Past time):

(1) I wish I had been there.
(2) She wishes she hadn't come here ever.
(3) They wish they hadn't come this dusty place.
(4) I wish if I had been there. (adv.cl)
(5) If only I hadn't seen him. (Principal Clause is omitted)
(6) If only you had been mine, O selfish heart!
(7) If only you had been my husband.

(C) **Wish + would/should + Action Words** (We are not happy about the situation now & we wish it would change in the future):

(1) I wish he would come one day.
(2) He wishes he would go from my life; O tragedy to bear thereafter!
(3) He wishes he would go; I like to give him 'welcome'.
(4) Jane wishes my dear friends would learn English from this page as well.
(5) I wish to be a lesbian; male hearts are too cruel!!
(6) If only he wouldn't do that.

53. Sometimes, particularly in language & literature, conjunctions are often omitted or understood. Here, such examples are:

1) I wished he would figure out I wanted to cry.
   - I wished ***(that)*** he would figure out ***(that)*** I wanted to cry.
2) Baba looked; I had stabbed him.
   - Baba looked ***like/as*** I had stabbed him.
3) I am sure, I had had a rank, he would have stood up, shook hands with me.
   - I am sure if I had had a rank, ***(that)*** he would have stood up, ***and*** shook hands with me.

6. The Mood (or the manner of expression)

54. Mood: Mood that denotes the state of verbs (how it is used in the sentence) and this defines the manner of expression of the speaker. It tells us about the state of a verb cum sentence in which state it is, what it expresses. It tells us thus, which is ***a statement*** or ***a question***, or ***an order*** or ***command, prayer, wish*** or ***hope,*** made or represented by the form of verb. Thus, a Verb may be in the following three main states which defines different functions of verbs. The three main states of a verb are:

- Indicative,
- Imperative &
- Subjunctive

Note: Where a **case** defines the state of a Noun, a **mood** defines the states of a verb which again defines the function of a sentence. Where there is no verb, expressed or implied, there is no life in a sentence.

The secondary auxiliary verbs are called modals, for they define the mood of a verb in a sentence.

(A) Indicative: The **Mood** denotes a statement, question, or a supposition, taken as a fact to happen—is called **Indicative Mood.** It is used-

1) To **state a fact** (the function of assertive sentence)
2) To **ask question** (interrogative)
3) To **express supposition which is taken as a fact**. (**may** or **must** happen)

(B) Imperative: The **mood** denotes order or command, threats or warn, request, advice or express prayer—is called **Imperative Mood.** It is used-

1) To **give order or command,**
2) To **threaten or to warn**,
3) To **make request or implore**,
4) To **give advice or exhort** *(try hard to persuade)*,
5) To **express entreaty or prayer**.

(C) Subjunctive: The Mood of the verb that expresses a wish or hope, desire, intention, or the resolution, purpose, condition or supposition (unreal to happen or hardly to be a fact) is called the **Subjunctive Mood**. Thus, it is used to express-

1) In certain traditional phrases, **to express a wish or hope**, (with exclamation at the end.) (**subject+be/v1**)
2) **To express desire, intention, or resolution**. (**be+v3**)
3) After the verb **'wish'** to **indicate supposition which is unreal or contrary to fact**.
4) After **'if', 'as if', 'as though', 'had+subject+ been'** to indicate unreality and improbability.
5) After **'It is time+subject+v2,** to imply that 'it is already late.
6) After **would rather+subject+v2**, to indicate preference.

The state of verbs in conditional clauses fall to the subjunctive mood. If already studied conditional & wish clauses, the subjunctive mood is easy realized.

Verb forms in Indicative Mood

55. Study the examples of verb in Indicative Mood in the sentences:

1) He goes. He does not go.
2) Rama goes to school daily.
3) Is she ill? Do you like tea?
4) Have you discovered it?

5) If he goes there, he will be punished. (The supposition is '*he will be punished*' & that is taken as a fact to happen in relation to the condition, '*if he goes there*')
6) If it rains, you must not come. (The fact is '*you must not come*' & it's based on the condition '*if it rains*'.)
7) When my parents were away, my grandmother would take care of me.
8) He'd always be the first to offer his help.
9) He is a would-be actor.

- **Supposed to be fact or true— fall to Indicative Mood,** but if such ones are not supposed to be a fact or to be true or which are improbable, they fall to the Subjunctive mood of the verb or sentence.

- **'would-be'** is an adjective, always used before a noun, meaning '*who is learning*, *under training* or *struggling to be; as,*)

10) Thapa is a would-be doctor. (He is under training)
11) Shilpa is a would-be nurse. (She would be a nurse, if she completes her course finally; a supposition which is taken as a fact.)
12) Taniya is a would-be sister. (Related medical or church)
13) Rana is a would-be collector.
14) Rohan is a would-be banker.
15) An advice for would-be parents. (for parents who hope to become father or mother soon)

- '**Would be**' is also used as the conditional past of 'will be':

16) He said he would be here at eight o'clock.
17) She asked if I would help her.
18) They told me that they probably wouldn't come.
19) She burned the letter, so that her husband would never read them.
20) She rings the bell, so that her pet dogs would hear & come for her help.
21) She would not change it, even though she knew it was wrong.
22) It would not work, even though we poured petrol into it.

- Used to say also what we like, love, hate, etc.:

23) I'd love coffee. I'd not like tea.

24) I'd not like tea in every half an hour.
25) I'd be only too glad to help.
26) I'd hate you to think you were criticizing me.
27) I'd rather come with you.
28) I'd you rather come with me.

- Imagine, say, think which are to be fact, not only imagination:

29) I'd imagine the job will take two days.
30) I'd say he was about fifty.

31) She doesn't think she'll get a job.
32) She should worry with all her qualifications. (ironical)
33) She doesn't need to worry.
34) Should anyone call (if anyone call), please tell them I'm busy.
35) He asked what time he should come.
36) I said that I should be glad to help.
37) Does he read? Are you a student?
38) Have you bought a camera?

- **Exception:**
- If **'would'** is used for talking about the result of an action or event that you merely imagine, hope or desire, but not to come as fact, as it is too late, or the condition is not going to happen, as the following, it is said to be in the '**Subjunctive Mood**'; as,

→ She'd look better with shorter hair. (Hardly possible she would trim her hair.)
→ If you went to see him, he would be delighted. (The condition didn't happen or took place, so his becoming 'delighted' is not now possible, at least for that reason.)
→ Get up! It would be a shame to miss the train. (It is taken, already the train is missed by them.)
→ She'd be a fool to accept it. (If she accepted, but that didn't happen)
→ If I had seen the advertisement in time, I would have applied for the job.
→ They would never have met if she had not gone to Emma's party.

Verb forms in Imperative Mood

Read examples of Mood- Imperative in the following sentences:

As it is used-

- To give order or command,
- To threaten or warn,
- To make request or implore,
- To give advice or exhort (try hard to persuade),
- To express entreaty or prayer.

⌘ The sentences are:

1) **Come** here. **March** on. **Let** him **go**.
2) **Move**, or you die. (Unless you move, you'll die: Indicative)
3) **May I come** in, sir? **Please give** me the book, I need it very urgent.
4) You **should not tell** lies. **Read**, and you **learn** (If you read, you'll learn: Indicative.).
5) **Have mercy** upon us. Give us our daily bread.
6) You **should not drink** and **drive**.
7) We **should be** more careful.
8) A present for me? You **should not have**! (Used to express 'thanks' to somebody politely)
9) You **should stop worrying** about it.
10) **Should I call** him & apologize? (Asking for advice)

⌘ **Note-1:** The Imperative Mood can strictly be used in the second person, **'spoken to'**. But in the **first & third person, a like sense** is expressed by the use of the auxiliary verb**, 'Let'.**

⌘ **Note-2: The subject of a verb** in the imperative mood **(you) is usually omitted**. Read through the examples.

11) ***Let*** me ***go***. (I want to go.)
12) ***Let*** him ***do***. (He is willing to do.)
13) ***Let*** her ***sing*** and dance. (She is willing...)
14) ***Open*** your book at page no 379.
15) ***Take care*** of your health.
16) ***Try*** to do better.
17) We ***should arrive*** before dark.
18) I ***should have finished*** the book by Friday.
19) In order that training should be effective it ***must be planned*** systemically.

20) She recommended that I ***should take*** some time off.
21) I wish you'd be quiet ***shut up*** for a minute.
22) Let's me think what the next we ***should do***.
23) ***Would*** you ***mind*** leaving us alone for a few minutes?
24) ***Would*** you ***open*** the door for me, please?
25) ***Would*** you ***like*** a sandwich?
26) ***Would*** you ***have dinner*** with us on Friday?
27) In case you ***should need*** any help, here is my number.
28) ***Should*** I ***go***? What ***should*** they ***do*** in that situation?
29) ***Should*** we ***help*** her, she misbehaved in the last time.
30) Save me. ***Help***! ***Have pity*** on us!

Verb forms in Subjunctive Mood

56. The Mood- Subjunctive which express-a wish or hope, desire, intention, or the resolution, purpose, condition or supposition (not a fact) **has two forms in its credit**:

A) Present Subjunctive, &
B) Past Subjunctive.

Note-1: Kindly follow the table:

Present Subjunctive		Past Subjunctive	
'Be' Verb	**Other Verbs**	**'Be' Verb**	**Other Verbs**
I be	I speak	I were	I spoke
We be	We speak	We were	We spoke
You be	You speak	You were	You spoke
(S)he be	She speak (not 'speaks')	(S)he were	(S)he spoke
They be	They speak	They were	They spoke
Arrangement of words in Present Subjunctive		**Arrangement of words in Past Subjunctive**	
Subject+be	Subject+base form of verb (V1)	Subject+were	Subject+past form of verb (V2)

(No Passive)	Be+3rd form of Verb (in Passive)	Had+subject+been (in passive form)	(No Passive)

57. Arrangement of Words in Present Subjunctive

1) **May/if + Subject + be** (to express a wish or hope, without exclamation at the end.)
   - **May she be** happy.
   - **If it be** (**not**: is) sin to work hard, I am a sinner.

2) **to express wish, hope or desire (as in Optative Sentence) with 'should be' + '-ing' or 3rd form of verb; as**
   - The roads ***should be less crowded*** today. (We hope so, though hardly to happen)
   - It ***should be raining*** now, according to the weather forecasting. (It was expecting, but not happened really)

3) **Subject + base form of verb (V1)[other than 'be' verb] / V1+subject** (to express a wish or hope, with exclamation at the end.)
   - **God bless** you!
   - **Heaven help** us!
   - Long **live the king!**

4) **Be+3rd form of Verb (in Passive)** (to express desire, intention or resolution of the speaker.)
   - I move that Mr. Gupta **be appointed** the Chairman.
   - We recommend that the subscription **be increased** to ten rupees.
   - It is suggested that an over pool **be built** to relieve the jam of the city.

58. More Examples of Present Subjunctive

1) Long ***live*** our struggle! Long ***live*** the king!
2) ***May*** they ***be*** happy. ***May*** she ***have*** a better groom.
3) If he ***wants, I'll do*** for him. If you ***want***, ***I'll do*** never.
4) The train ***should have arrived*** 30 minutes ago.

5) What ***would*** you ***do***, if something else ***happened*** to you then? (The thing did not happen; past subjunctive)
6) If you ***should change*** of mind, do ***let me know***. (I already know she would not change her mind.)
7) We ***work*** that we ***may live***. (To mean purpose)
8) She ***works hard*** that she ***may succeed***. (purpose)
9) Work and you ***will succeed***. Touch it, and you die.
10) I ***warn*** you ***lest*** you ***should*** fail.
11) ***Follow*** me, or you'll ***be punished***.
12) If he ***be*** there, he ***will help*** you.

Note: A lot of subjunctive similar statements that tend to be fact fall to Indicative Mood; so why, presently Subjunctive tends to be merged with Indicative Mood. However, as still exist, carry on with its features and examples to be used separately.

59. Arrangement of Words in Past Subjunctive

1) Subject+wish+subject+were/v2

- **I wish I knew** his name. **I wish this were** possible.
- **I wish I were** a millionaire. **I wish I were** an eagle.
- **She wishes the car belonged** to me.
- I **wish I had** the virtues.

2) If+subject+were/v2

- ***If I, were*** you (i.e., *but I am not you*), I should do it.
- I would go there, **if I were** you (*but I was not*)
- **If he were** (not was), he would have come.
- ***If we started*** now, we would be in time. (*But we didn't start yet*)

3) As if+subject+were/v2

- He orders me about ***as if I were*** his wife. (*But I am not*).
- She pretends as if she were dead.
- She acted her role as if she was the bandit.

4) As though+subject+were/v2

- He walks ***as though he were*** drunk. (*But he is not*).
- He sang as though his mother were in hospital. (*But not really*)
- He failed as though he were not in the classes for long. (*he was present in the classes*)
-

5) After **would rather,** use **'you'** or **'he'** as **subject& v2**, to indicate preference.

- I ***would rather*** you went by air (*I **should prefer** you to go by air*).
- They ***would rather* you paid** (*should prefer you to pay*) them by cheque.
- I would rather she took divorced from the cruel man.

6) **Had+subject+been+participle/adj/adv/noun complement**
   - ***Had he been*** present (*i.e., but he was not*), he would oppose you.
   - **Had I been** there (*but I was not*), I would save her from them.
   - **Had she been** my wife, what the fuck she would do?

7) **It is time+subject+v2/progressive form** with **'were'** with all persons and number; as,
   - **It is time** we started. *(Implying, we are already late)*
   - **It is time** we were eating.
   - **It is time** she were giving lecture in the classes.

60. More Examples of Past Subjunctive

1) ***Were he here*** *(if he was present here, but he was not)*, I ***would*** tell him this. I ***wish*** that he ***would*** pass.
2) ***I wish I were*** a millionaire. ***Wish*** that ***he were*** here.
3) ***I wish I were*** a bird. I ***wish*** the ***thief were*** punished.
4) She ***wishes the house belonged*** to you.

- (wish + subject + past form of verb/were)
- Indirectly, subjunctive mood can also be used to give advice; as,

5) I ***would*** not drink, ***if I were*** you. *(The mood is subjunctive, as it is not true, you would not be me & I would never be you.)*
6) I ***should*** wait a little longer, ***if I were*** you.
7) ***Would*** that he ***had lived*** to see it. *(Expressing strong wish, but it would never be happened, because he is already dead)*
8) ***If I were*** asked to work on Sundays, I ***should*** resign.
9) ***If I were*** a bird, I ***would*** fly in the sky.
10) ***If he should*** come, I ***should*** go. (a mere or unreal supposition that didn't happen)

11) He ***went*** there so that he ***might see*** the sight. (purpose)

Note: The difference of Indicative & Subjunctive in case of supposition or condition is, one is fact, and another is in imaginary merely.

7. Classification of Sentence, based on Functions

61. What is a Sentence: A group of words, with at least one subject & one finite verb that makes a complete sense.

We can define it another way.

The term 'sentence'-

- consists of a group of words;
- It contains a subject & at least a finite verb (or 'a unit of finite verb');
- May consist of one or more Phrases;
- It may consist of one or more Clauses;
- Have a complete sense.
- Begins with a capital letter & ends with- . /? /! marks.
- It is the largest structural unit of a language, while a word is the smallest.

62. A sentence does different functions to express sense of the speaker. It may be used to give information, to ask questions, to give order, request, advice, or command as well as it may express a wish, hope, desire, blessing or prayer. On account of these multi functions of a sentence, sentences are divided or grouped into the following five kinds. Have a quick look at the PowerPoint slide:

63. Assertive Sentence: **That states a fact** or **makes an assertion** or **a statement**, usually begins with a subject & ends with a full stop (.), is called an Assertive Sentence or Statement. Sometimes, examples are more effective to understand than mere illustrations. So, study the following examples and guess their functions:

1) Humpty Dumpty sat on a wall.
2) The cow is a useful animal.
3) It is worshipped in Hindu religion.
4) He is my best friend.
5) Hope (I hope), you will pass the examination.
6) Rabindra Nath was a Bengali Poet.
7) He was also a novelist, short-story writer and an excellent composer of songs, besides a singer.
8) The boys are not reading at any school.
9) Yes, I can do the job. No, I cannot do the job.

What did you notice in them? What functions did they do in the sentences? Are they as the followings?

Functions	Sentences
1) To describe a situation or an event, or to give introduction:	1) There is a small river, Atreyee, which pass through the town, Balurghat. Peter lives here from long past when he wore half pant.
2) To narrate a thing:	2) Teacher said that Darjeeling is the queen of hill. Mr. Peter is a teacher.
3) To give information or reporting:	3) India won the last World Cup.
4) Asserting a fact:	4) Yes, I can do the job.
5) Denying a fact:	5) No, I can't do the job.
6) Illustrating:	6) Some of the best poets of our time are A, B & C.
7) Describing a process:	7) The preparation of teas goes through a number of stages.
8) Stating a cause, result, purpose, etc.:	8) She cannot attend the school because of her illness. He worked hard, so he passed. He had worked hard, so that he could pass.

64. Interrogative Sentence: A sentence that asks a question, *begins with a helping verb or wh. word & ends with a question mark(?), is called an* Interrogative Sentence or Question; as,

1) Does she like tea or coffee? What is today's menu?
2) Where do you live? Who is our best friend?
3) What is in your mind? Can't we live alone?
4) Did he write any novel? What is his name?
5) Is he really a writer? Have you read his any novel?
6) What are you reading? Why is the woman shouting?
7) Can he swim? Will they come today?
8) Does she not read at any school?
9) Why do wives quarrel with their husbands?
10) Why do we fall in love with women or beautiful girls thousand times?

An Interrogative sentence do the following functions:

Functions	Sentences
1) To ask questions,	1) What is your name? Why were you absent from school?

enquiring or asking for information:	2) Who doesn't want money? (To get reply 'everyone wants') Who is not scared of devil? ('everyone is scared of')
2) Asserting:	
3) Ask for help, requesting, or seeking permission:	3) Would you please help me to come out of this worse situation? Will you please call a doctor? I need an immediate treatment. May I come in, sir?
4) Ask for opinion or advice:	4) What should we do, will you suggest for anything?
5) Expressing doubt, etc.:	5) Who knows when rain will stop? (uncertain). Are you a man? (No, a devil.)

65. Imperative Sentence: <u>That expresses a command (order), an entreaty (request), or an advice and similar things;</u> where the subject (you) is left out or understood, is called an Imperative Sentence. An imperative <u>may end with</u> ***full stop*** or ***question mark*** at the end. Study the examples:

1) Be quiet. Have mercy upon us.
2) Will you pass the tray, please?
3) Please give me the pen.
4) Sit and study your lesson.
5) Write this essay within five hundred words.
6) I wish you write it for me. (Request; or an order, politely asked)
7) Lend me your bicycle. Finish it within ten minutes.
8) Do not sit on the desk. You should not be there alone.

Study the functions of Imperative sentence in the chart, given below:

Functions	Sentences
1) Order, commanding, or instructing:	1) Stop talking. Soldiers, march ahead; we can't stay here long. Do the job as I say.
2) appealing, or entreating:	2) Please give me a piece of bread. Please, don't accept my love; I am a devil in heart.

3) Permitting:	3) You may smoke, but your lunch is at your own risk. Yes, you may come in; but here is none.
4) Prohibiting:	4) Do not smoke here. You can't go there. Don't make a noise.
5) Advising:	5) Do not idle away your invaluable time, or you will have no time even to repent.
6) Suggesting or seek for suggestions:	6) Let me explain the matter. Let's go for a picnic. We should celebrate the occasion.
7) Reminding:	7) Kindly remember the date of wedding.

66. Optative Sentence: **A sentence that expresses a desire, wish, prayer or blessing**, is called an Optative Sentence. An Optative may end with a **full stop** or **exclamation** (!). An exclamation is used with the desire or wish that is not real (Study subjunctive mood). The modals – **may, should**, & the verb **wish, were** – are vastly used in this kind of sentences; as,

1) May you live long. May God bless you.
2) I wish you soon be cured. I wish you to be cured.
3) I wish you should be cured soon.
4) May you not win the race.
5) If I were a bird! If I had been a millionaire!
6) May the girl sing well. May the old man have peace.
7) I wish you must grow up soon. (Wish or prayer: 'I want you to grow up soon.')

Study the functions of Optative that do in the sentence:

Functions	Sentences
1) To express **Wish** or **Desire:**	1) I wish you a long life. If I were a bird! If I had been a billionaire! If I had two wings! I wish I were taller than my love!
2) Expressing **Prayer:**	2) Long live the king. May you live long. May God bless you. May everyone's son flourish in life. **May she be** happy.
3) Giving **Curse:**	3) May she live long, and feel the pain of old age by firsthand experience.
4) To express **Blessing:**	4) May God protect you from all dangers. **God bless** you! **May Heaven help** you in all!

67. **Exclamatory Sentence:** **A sentence that expresses a sudden feeling or emotion** due to *wonder, fear, approval, or compliment*, etc., usually ends with an exclamation after interjection, and a full stop (.) at end of the sentence, is called an Exclamatory Sentence (that expresses exclamation; strong feelings). The words of Interjection like, – **bravo, hurrah, well-done** & other parts of speech like, **hear, how, what, shocking, strange**– are often used in the exclamatory sentences. Study the examples:

a. **Well done friend!** You have done excellent.
b. **Good bye!** We don't know will we meet again?
c. **O dear me!** What you have done.
d. **Bad luck to it!** He had tried his best yet.
e. **Hear!** What a song she sings.
f. **Strange!** She went there.
g. **How** vary kind of you!
h. **How** beautiful!
i. **Shocking!** How she can say so.

- The words which are generally used in an exclamatory sentence to express strong emotion or feelings are called the Interjections. For more such words, study the chapter of **Interjections.**

j. **How cold** the night is!
k. **What a shame**!
l. **Hush!** The teacher is coming.
m. **Oh!** What a beautiful scene.
n. **How beautiful** the bird is!
o. **What!** He can't swim.
p. **Wow!** He read excellent. It sounds like a song.
q. **Shame!** She doesn't leave even her boss!

Study the functions, Exclamatory do in the sentence:

Functions	Sentences
1) Expressing wonder 2) Expressing joy	1) What a grand hotel is this! 2) Hurrah! I have completed the project. 3) Alas! I am undone in life.

3) Expressing grief	4) Oh! You have failed. I am sorry.
4) Expressing pity	5) Phi! She did a devilish job. How untidy the room is!
5) Expressing disgust	6) Hello! My friend, we are meeting after long days.
6) Greeting	7) Bravo! Well done! What a shot he did. Carry on.
7) Encouraging	8) Good morning. Good evening. Good night.
8) Wish &	
9) Bid good-bye or farewell	9) Good-bye! We shall not meet again. / Bye! See you soon.
10) Make a taunt	10) Yea! You are a Shakespeare of our time.

68. One more functional category of sentence (rhetorical).

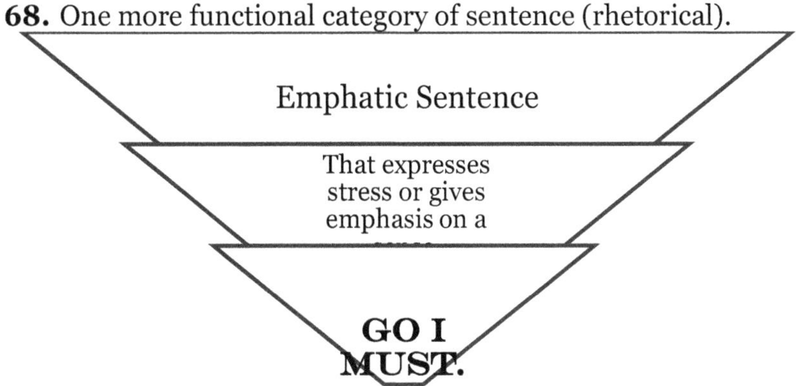

- **Explanation: 'Go I must.'** It means, 'I must go.' A simple Assertive sentence to express the certainty of his going or to give more emphasis on the sense, shifting the main verb 'go' or modal 'must' before the subject 'Must I go' (and often using 'do' before main verb; 'I do go there in time.')— is termed as the 'rhetorical use of exclamatory sentence'.

- An Emphatic sentence, actually, is a variation of Assertive or Exclamatory Sentence, made often by shifting the main verb before subject or use 'do or did' before the main verb (in assertive). Some more examples of such sentences are:

  a. **Go,** you must there in time. Don't worry.
  b. You **do** believe me I was not that man.
  c. **Must** you be a rascal (You must be a rascal.)
  d. **Killing him** you are a criminal! (You are a criminal by killing him.)

e. **Go,** you must go there. (Using double times, the main verb 'go'; first 'go' to give emphasis)
f. **Attend** you must be there. (You must attend there.)
g. **Dance** he did well on the stage.
h. **Hit** he the ball, excellent, like Sachin Tendulkar!
i. I **myself** did it. She **herself** went there. (Using a reflexive pronoun)
j. You yourself correct **first.** (Giving emphasis on the adverb 'first', using it at last; while it should be, **'First, you correct yourself'** in the assertive sentence.)
k. She **herself** loves. ('She merely loves herself.')

Formation of Affirmative & Negative Sentences

69. All the five or six (including emphatic, if we take it as a different kind, though I don't think so except to be a variation)—can be expressed in negative sense side by side as the affirmative sense of the sentence. Study the chart:

Sentence in Affirmative way	*Sentence in Negative sense*
1. I know you. (*Assertive*) 2. Will you go? (*Interrogative*) 3. Come at once. (*Imperative*) 4. God might save him. (*Optative*) 5. How foolish! (*Exclamatory*) 6. Must I go. (*Emphatic*)	1. I don't know the person. (*Assertive*) 2. Have you not finished this? (*interrogative*) 3. Don't run in the sun. (*Imperative*) 4. May God not forgive his sin. (*Optative*) 5. Is he not a fool, doing like this! (*Exclamatory*) 6. Must you not do it. (*Emphatic*)

- 'Affirmative' means **that affirms something**; & 'negative of the sense' means **that denies something**. Thus, each kind of sentence can be expressed either in affirmative or negative sense.
- In the above, the sentences (in the affirmative column & in the negative column) are different in meaning & expression from each

other; as the followings:

- → You went there. = You didn't go there.
- → Will you like tea? = Wil you not like tea?
- → Do it. = Don't do it.
- → God bless you. = God might not forget your sin. (God may not bless you.).
- → How you can do it! = How can't you do it (such an easy task)!
- → Go I must there. = Must not I go there.

- In all the above cases the sentences are converted from affirmative to negative, and their sense have also been changed. For this conversion of sense and sentence, study the following chart of <u>adverbs (mainly) to form Negation and Affirmation</u>.

The Words of Negation & Affirmation

(adverbs or compounds)

18

Words of Negation	Words of Affirmation
No, Not, Never, No longer, No more, Nothing, Not a bit, Nobody/None/ No one,	One, any, all, some, ever, always, anybody, somebody,
Nowhere, Nothing but, Scarcely, Hardly, Rarely=15	Everyone, someone, something, anything somewhere, anywhere = (14)

- How to form negative sentences with the help of words of Negation, study the following chart. However, more details in the allotted chapter:

How to form negative sentences-

1) By 'Do' helping verb	• He reads a book. = He **does not** read a book.

(do/does/did + not)	• They run a race. = They **do not** run.
2) By other auxiliaries— ('Be', 'Have' & Modal verb+ no/not)	• We are going. = We **are not** going. • They were sailors. = They **were not** sailors. • I have a bi-cycle. = I **have no** bi-cycle. • You can do it now. = You **canno**t do it now. • We shall visit there. = We **shall not** visit the place.
3) By some Adverbs, besides no, not: — (Nobody, none, no one, never, nothing, nowhere, scarcely, hardly and to keep sense, retained, use of antonyms of main words, along with negation.)	• I always remember you. = I **never** forget you. • There were so many people. = There were **none**. • It will be distributed to everyone. = It will be distributed to **none**. /**no one** • I want everything. = I want/decline **nothing**. • God is everywhere. = **No one** can say God is **nowhere**. • I liked my friend very much. = I **hardly** disliked my friend.

How to form affirmative sentences from negative-

1) By omitting 'do/does/did not' & 'no' or 'not' Adverb from the sentence	I do not like it. > I like it. You have no car. > You have a car.
2) By use of (adverbs)— (Ever, always, anybody, all, every one, anyone, anywhere, everywhere etc.)	I **never** forget you. >I **always** remember you. I hate **none**. >I love **everyone**.
3) **By antonym**	She **loves** me **not**. > She **hates** me.

How to form interrogative sentences-

1) **By use of 'Do' verb:** (Do/Does/Did+ Sub.+ Main Verb+ Obj.+ Others)	Rita sang a sweet song. = **Did** Rita sing a song? He reads a novel. = **Does** he read any? I apology to you. = **Do** you apology me?
2) By use of other Helping or Modal Auxiliaries: (H.V./M.V.+ Sub.+ Main Verb+ Obj.+ Others)	I am reading a book. = **Are** you reading? She has done her task. =**Has** she done her task? You will be there? = **Will** you be? You may come in.= **May** I come in, sir?
3) **In case of "Wh' words:** ('Wh'+ H.V./ M.V.+Sub.+ Main Verb+ Obj.+ Others)	I went to Kolkata. = **Where did** you go? I am eating rice. = **What are** you eating? I have a car. = **What do** you have? He had gone there to meet her. = **Why had** he gone there?

8. Classification of Sentence, based on Structure

70. Here is the 2nd way of Classification of Sentences. This time it is based on Structure / Construction / Clauses.

Based on Clauses, Sentences are of three kinds:

A. **Simple Sentence**,
B. **Compound Sentence** &
C. **Complex Sentence**.

- Read the slide:

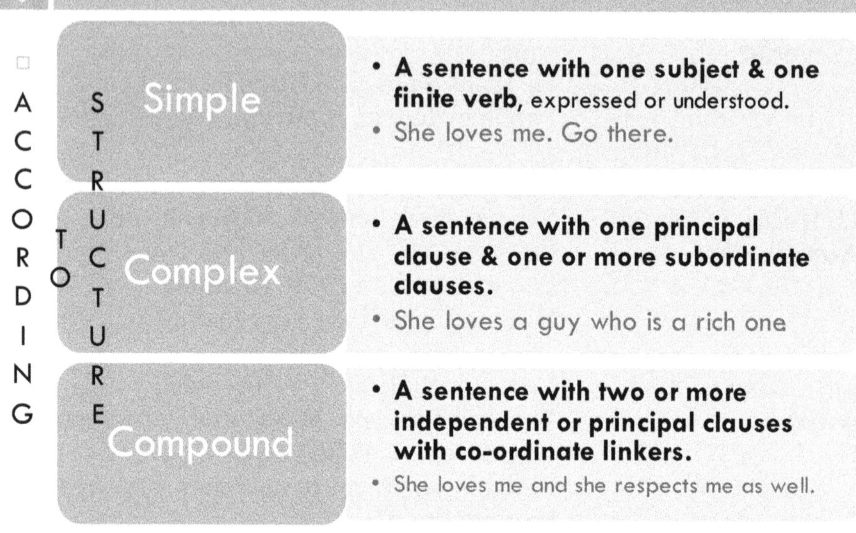

⌘ <u>Explanation:</u>

A. **Simple Sentence**: A sentence in which there is only one principal clause **(i.e., one subject & one finite Verb)**. Read the examples:

1) His courage won him honor.
2) She turned to me.
3) I decided to stick to the agenda.
4) Your husband might have killed Zara Lone.
5) He had a clear motive.
6) Two whistles are enough for the signal.
7) She fought with me for a year.
8) She loved you a lot too, Keshav.
9) Why women's love is invisible to us?
10) Seven people raised their glasses high in the air.

B. **Compound Sentence**: A compound sentence is formed of <u>at least one principal</u> & <u>one co-ordinate clause.</u>

Sometimes, it is said a compound sentence is composed of two or more principal clauses; whereas, a principal clause is connected with a co-ordinate conjunction. Read the definition:

- A sentence with two or more independent or principal clauses with or without any sub-ordinate clause joined together by co-ordinate conjunctions, is called the **Compound Sentence**.

- The following Co-ordinate Conjunctions are generally used to form Co-ordinate clauses and Compound Sentences:

(1) And, also, too, as well as, both—and, not only—but also, etc. (meaning cumulative or addition of word, phrase, clause of equal rank);

1) We carved not a line, **and** we raised not a stone.
2) God made the country **and** man-made the town.
3) Vishal & Virat are good bowlers. (Vishal is a good bowler & Virat is a good bowler.)

(2) Either...or, neither...nor, or, else etc. (that refer selection or alternation between two);

4) She must weep, **or** she will die. **Either** he is mad, **or** he feigns madness.
5) Is that story true **or** false? **Neither** a borrower, **nor** a lender be.
6) We can travel by land **or** water. They toil not, **neither** do they spin.
7) **Either** you are mistaken, **or** I am. Walk quickly, **else** you will not overtake him.

(3) Still, yet, only, but, however, nevertheless, whereas, though —yet, etc. (meaning adversative or contrast between two or more);

8) Our hoard is little, ***but*** our hearts are great.
9) The man is poor, ***but*** honest. (The man is poor, but he is honest.)
10) He is slow, ***but*** he is sure. I was annoyed, ***still*** I kept quiet.
11) I would come; ***only*** that I am engaged. He was all right; ***only*** he was fatigued.

(4) Therefore, for, so, then, so then etc. (meaning Illative or Inference; coming to conclusion).

12) Something certainly fell in; ***for*** I heard a splash.

13) All precautions must have been neglected, ***for*** the plague spread rapidly.

Above all the examples are the examples of using **Co-ordinate Conjunctions** to form **Co-ordinate Clauses;** and thus, they are (the sentences) are also the examples of **Compound Sentences**. **However, point to remember:** Co-ordinate Conjunctions are used not always to make Compound Sentences, but bare Simple sentences too.

71. When two or more subjects joined by '**and**' & they are **inseparable** denoting a single fact, one is incomplete without the other, or the thing will not be made at all, the sentence is not a Compound but a Simple Sentence.

The following are not Compound sentences, though used Co-ordinates; as,

1. She **and** I are great friends.
2. The PM **and** MPs agreed to pass the bill.
3. Meera **and** Anjali are walking together.
4. Curry **and** rice is my favorite dish.
5. The sum **and** substance of this story is poor.
6. Two **and** two make four.
7. Bread **and** milk is a wholesome food.

The above look like compound, but they are not, as subjects are inseparable. The subject formed by co-ordinate cannot be broken up. The two here make a single fact. Without one, other is invalid to mean. They are examples of Simple Sentences.

72. How to find a Compound Sentence

A Compound sentence must have **at least one Principal and one Co-ordinate Clause** (Co-ordinate clause means = Principal Clause with Co-ordinate Conjunction) & may have any number of sub-ordinate clauses or not at all; as,

1) The moon was bright ***and*** we could see our way.
2) Night came on ***and*** rain fell heavily ***and*** we got very wet.
3) Anil called at 5.30 ***and*** I told him that you had gone out.

4) I shall do it now ***or*** I shall not do it at all.
5) He gave them no money ***nor*** he did help them anyway.
6) He threw the stone ***but*** it missed the target.
7) He ***neither*** obtains success ***nor*** deserves it.
8) He is ***either*** a mad ***or*** has the mentality of a criminal.
9) I both thanked him ***and*** rewarded him.
10) They love & torture, they love torture & love. –Peter.
11) I am ill, ***but*** I shall go.
12) I went there ***and*** (I) found that my brother was ill.
13) The book which you gave me was a good one, ***but*** I have lost it.
14) Man is guided by reason, ***and*** beast by instinct.
15) The horse reared ***and*** the rider was thrown.
16) I called him, ***but*** he gave me no answer.
17) ***Either*** he is drowned ***or*** some passing ship has saved him.
18) He rushed into the field, ***and*** foremost fighting fell.
19) Man proposes, ***but*** God disposes.
20) Listen carefully ***and*** take notes.

73. Compound Sentence is used to avoid needless repetition of same words ***by contraction*** or ***giving shortened form***, or ***letting them understood*** in the following way-

a) With two or more predicates are for one subject:
   - **He** came and (**he**) delivered a lecture.
   - ***I*** was pleased but ***(I)*** could not do anything.

b) For two or more subjects there is one predicate:
   - They (**are wrong**) as well as you **are wrong**.
   - Either he (**must go**) or his brother **must go**.
   - He **is** poor but (he **is**) honest.

74. Relative Pronouns or Adverbs may also form Compound Sentences, besides Sub-ordinate Relative clause and complex sentence. Study the following:

Generally Relative Pronouns and Relative Adverbs do function of Sub-ordinate Conjunctions and they form Complex Sentences, but with the following they do form co-ordinate meanings, and thereby they have formed Compound Sentences:

1) He helped me, **which** (=and this/it) was very kind of him.
2) I went to Kolkata, **where** (=and there) I stayed for one month.
3) I went to the Principal, **who** (=and he) spoke kindly to me.

4) At last, I found him, **which** (=and this) relieved me of my anxiety.
5) They arranged for a priest, **who** (=and he) offered a ten-thousand – rupee package for the cremation.

When **relative pronouns or adverbs are used as co-ordinate conjunctions, they should be separated by comma from the principal clauses,** unless they are taken to be sub-ordinate conjunctions and the sentences are the complex sentences, in place of compound; as,

- I went to Kolkata where I stayed for a month. ('the place where I stayed')
- I went to Kolkata which is the capital of West Bengal.

The last two sentences are the examples of Complex Sentence.

Complex Sentence

C. **Complex Sentence:** A complex sentence is formed of one principal & at least one sub-ordinate clause.

Definition:

- The sentence with at least one Sub-ordinate clause and at least one Principal Clause, is called the Complex Sentence.

- A clause with Sub-ordinate conjunctions is called sub-ordinate clause, and the clause may be **a Noun Clause, Relative** or **Adjective Clause,** or an **Adverbial Clause.** A Sub-ordinate clause in collaboration with a Principal Clause builds a Complex Sentence; as the following:
  - I thought of Raghab who was at that moment was attending a party.
  - She gave me the same feeling (that) she gave me last.

75. Whether a sentence is complex or compound—how to find out?

It is determined by the combination of Principal clause with at least one Sub-ordinate or Co-ordinate Clause in the sentence.

- A Complex sentence must have **at least one Principal and one Sub-ordinate Clause** (Sub-ordinate clause means = Principal Clause with Sub-ordinate Conjunction or Relative Pronoun or Relative Adverb, etc.). A complex sentence may have more than one sub-ordinate clauses which may also be joined by co-ordinate conjunctions; as,

- **The boy** who came here yesterday and whom you must have seen **is my brother.** (In the sentence, there is one Principal clause 'The boy is my brother' & two Sub-ordinate clauses which are joined by a co-ordinate conjunction 'and'. The sentence is Complex Sentence.)

- As he is ill, and (as) the doctor has advised him for rest, **he cannot come to welcome you.** (Here also the two sub-ordinate clauses are joined by a co-ordinate conjunction 'and', but the sentence is the Complex sentence. It has one Principal & two sub-ordinate clauses.)

76. More examples of Complex Sentences:

1) They rested **when** evening came.
2) **As** the boxers advanced into the ring, the people said they would not allow them to fight.
3) **If** the news made you uncomfortable, the proof will make you even more so.
4) After my uncle arrived, they took over the cremation.
5) Even though he had died, I felt the fire must hurt him.
6) I remembered how he would dress me up for school when I was a child.

- Let's have a revision of some pages from the chapter of Sub-ordinate Conjunctions to understand better the Sub-ordinate Clauses as well as the Complex Sentences.

77. Know the Functions of Sub-ordinate Conjunctions that join clauses (adverbial) which express:

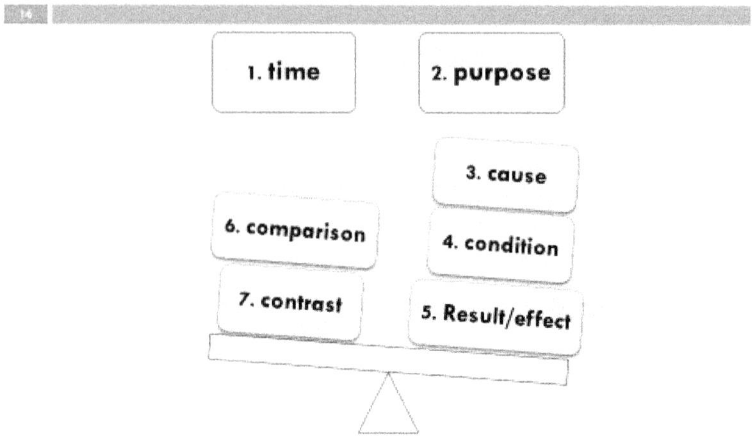

Let's see now the Conjunctions & their Functions they do in the sentences:

Adverbial function of conjunction	Examples of conjunction
Time	After, before, since, as soon as, while, until, as, as long as, till...
Purpose	In order that, lest, so that, that...
Cause	because, since, as, for,
Condition	provided, supposing, unless, as, if, whether,
Result/Effect	so...that, that,
Comparison	than, as...as
Contrast	Though, although, however, even if.

- Sub-ordinate Conjunctions cum Sub-ordinate Clauses do the following functions in Complex sentences. Study the examples:

(1) **Conjunctions that refer 'Time':**

1) We arrived **after** you had gone.
2) I waited **till** the train arrived.
3) **When** you are called, you must come in at once.
4) Do not go **before** I come.
5) We got into the port **before** the storm came on.
6) I would die **before** I lied.
7) My grandfather died **before** I was born.
8) I will stay **until** you return.
9) Many things have happened **since** I saw you.
10) He returned home **after** I had gone.

(2) **Purpose:**

11) She must weep, **lest** she die.
12) We tried hard **in order that** it spin.
13) He is intelligent, **so** he feigned madness.
14) We eat **so that** we may live.
15) He held my hand **lest** I should fall.
16) She feigned madness, **so that** she saved herself from imminent danger.
17) We travel by land or water **so that** we can reach another place.

(3) **Cause or Reason:**

18) I cannot give you any money, **for** I have none.
19) **Since** you wish it, it shall be done.
20) He may enter **as** he is a friend.
21) **As** he was not there, I spoke to his brother.
22) I did not come **because** you did not call me.
23) He deserved to succeed, **for** he worked hard.

(4) **Condition:**

24) You will not succeed **unless** you work harder.
25) He fled **lest** he should be killed.
26) He asked **whether** he might have a holiday.
27) You will get the prize **if** you deserve it.
28) You will be late **unless** you hurry.
29) I shall be vexed **if** you do that.
30) Grievance cannot be redressed u**nless** they are known.
31) Give me to drink, **else** I shall die of thirst.
32) **If** I feel any doubt, I'll ask.
33) I shall go, **whether** you come or not.
34) He will sure to come **if** you invite him.
35) **Unless** you tell me the truth, I shall punish you.

(5) **Result/effect/Consequence:**

36) He worked very hard, **so that** he might pass.
37) He was so tired **that** he could scarcely stand.

(6) **Comparison:**

38) He is richer **than** I am.
39) He is **as** intelligent **as** Biram.
40) Tom runs faster **than** Harry.
41) The earth is larger **than** the moon.

(7) **Contrast / Concession:**

42) Our hoard is little, **but** our hearts are great.
43) The man is poor, **but** honest. (The man is poor, but he is honest.)
44) He is slow, **but** he is sure.
45) I was annoyed, **still** I kept quiet.
46) I would come; **only** that I am engaged.
47) He was all right; **only** he was fatigued.
48) I hear **that** your brother is in London.

78. The Interrogative Pronouns or Interrogative Adjectives, Relative Pronouns or Relative Adverbs (wh. words & that)—they also join sub-ordinate clauses (mainly Noun or Relative clauses) to form Complex Sentences; as the following:

1) He could trace his umbrella **which** was blue. (Relative Adj.; adj. or relative Clause).
2) He was surprised to see the man **that** was his own brother.
3) I do not know **why** she did not join us. (Reason—adv. clause)
4) I do not know **why** she had gone.
5) I do not know **where** she had gone. (Place—adv. clause)
6) He could trace his umbrella **where** he had left it.
7) She was the girl **whom** I loved immense. (Relative clause)
8) You are talking to the man **who** was my brother. (Relative clause)
9) I didn't know **that** she had gone. (Concession conj.)
10) Make hay **while** the sun shines.

79. Besides, Simple, Compound & Complex, there are <u>two more structural categories of sentences. Read their definitions:</u>

Complex Compound

- A sentence with one principal & two or more sub-ordinate clauses and ***where the sub-ordinate clauses*** **or** ***complex sentences are joined by a co-ordinate linker***. [Peter choices a term 'variation or a kind' of Complex, but not a separate kind of sentence, however]. You may read the examples:

1) **She loves her master** who is soft hearted ***and*** who has bright personality.
(The sentence has 1 principal, 2 sub-ordinates. However, the two sub-ordinates are joined by 'and' a conjunction. It is an example of **Complex Compound** Sentence.)

2) **I shall go there** when you come, ***but*** **(I shall) return** ***as soon as*** you leave the place.
(The sentence has 2 principals, 2 sub-ordinates. However, the two complex sentences are connected by 'but', a co-ordinate Conjunctions. It is an example of **Complex Compound** Sentence. The two complex sentences are joined by conjunction 'but'.)

3) As he is ill, **he cannot move out**, ***but*** **we expect** that he will come round before the ceremony ends.
(The sentence has 2 principals, 3 sub-ordinates. The two complex sentences are added by conjunction 'but'. It is also an example of Complex Compound Sentence)

4) **I am a professor** who teaches students in a college ***and*** **you are a high school teacher** who teaches his students at a school.

5) ***Either*** **he is an engineer** who works in the corporate ***or*** **he is the boss** who provides recruitments to the people like us.

Compound Complex

- A sentence with two or more principal clauses; when one is independent, the other is in the complex sentence and both (simple & complex) are joined by a co-ordinate conjunction, is called Compound Complex.

- [Peter choices a term 'variation or a kind' of Compound, but not a separate kind of sentence]. Read the examples:

  1) **She loves me** ***but*** as I am unattainable, **she loves you**.

2) **I am a teacher *and* you are a doctor** who treats patients at the hospital.

- In the above both sentences, there is one principal clause which is independent and it is joined by a complex sentence by a co-ordinate conjunction 'and'. So, it is compound and complex, Compound Complex.

About Mr. Peter

Mr. Peter is a penname of the writer, an Indian and a teacher in West Bengal. Most of his academic works are the products of his professional career what he held over twenty years and continuing… Mr. Peter loves to publish his books in the self-publishing platforms, like Amazon (worldwide) and notionpress.com (India). For this, Peter heartily pays his gratitude to Amazon, notionpress.com and for marketing to Flipkart, Amazon & different social media. Presently, Mr. Peter's books are available in 3 formats—eBook, Paperback & Hardcover. Mr. Peter's books which are published at Notion Press Pvt. Ltd., Chennai, are available to buy on **notionpress.com, Flipkart**, **Amazon**.in

Discounts, promotions, etc. are available in all platforms. However, if one seeks special offers for marketing or wants to give bulk order, s/he may visit only to **notionpress.com** (type **Mr. Peter** in the search box, and use following **Coupon Codes:** (If not work, for the current status, one may contact by https://www.facebook.com/profile.php?id=100081822070172 or (5) Books Campaigns, Free Coupons, Learning English Grammar & Composition | Facebook

notionpress.com/en/coupon_manager

books Author Dashboard My Shelf Mr Peter

Campaign Name	Book Name	Coupon Type	Discount %	Discounted Price	Used Count	Report	Actions
bulk01	Peter's 'English Grammar'	Bulk-Use	30	~~₹ 1201~~ ₹ 841	0/100	Download	Delete
unique01	Peter's 'English Grammar'	Multi-Use	23	~~₹ 1201~~ ₹ 925	0/100	Download	Delete
bulk00	A Book of Advanced Writing Skill, the Complete Version (incl Part-1, 2 & 3)	Bulk-Use	23	~~₹ 780~~ ₹ 601	1/100	Download	Delete
unique00	A Book of Advanced Writing Skill, the Complete Version (incl Part-1, 2 & 3)	Multi-Use	15	~~₹ 780~~ ₹ 663	0/100	Download	Delete
DEAL11	Development of Writing Skill, Part-3	Bulk-Use	24	~~₹ 365~~ ₹ 278	0/10	Download	Delete
PUJADEAL10	Development of Writing Skill, Part-3	Multi-Use	18	~~₹ 365~~ ₹ 300	0/10	Download	Delete
DEAL10	Development of Writing Skill, Part-2	Bulk-Use	24	~~₹ 365~~ ₹ 278	1/10	Download	Delete
PUJADEAL9	Development of Writing Skill, Part-2	Multi-Use	18	~~₹ 365~~ ₹ 300	0/10	Download	Delete
PujaDeal8	Steps to Composition (Development of Writing Skill, from Primary to Secondary Level)	Multi-Use	20	~~₹ 300~~ ₹ 240	1/10	Download	Delete
PujaDeal7	Rhetoric & Prosody	Multi-Use	20	~~₹ 240~~ ₹ 192	0/10	Download	Delete
PujaDeal6	Question Bank of English Grammar & Composition	Multi-Use	20	~~₹ 559~~ ₹ 448	0/10	Download	Delete
PujaDeal5	Study of Subject-Verb Agreement, Narration Change, Use of Punctuation; including Analysis, Synthesis & Split-up	Multi-Use	20	~~₹ 301~~ ₹ 241	0/10	Download	Delete
PujaDeal4	Detail Study of Phrases, Clauses & Sentences, including Idioms & Phrasal Verbs	Multi-Use	20	~~₹ 290~~ ₹ 232	0/10	Download	Delete
PujaDeal3	Study of Adverbs, Prepositions, Conjunctions & Interjections	Multi-Use	20	~~₹ 260~~ ₹ 208	0/10	Download	Delete

www.ingramcontent.com/pod-product-compliance
Ingram Content Group UK Ltd.
Pitfield, Milton Keynes, MK11 3LW, UK
UKHW022020190726
13853UKWH00005B/2026

9 798887 045825